3/12

A taste of
OXFORD
INSPIRED RECIPE IDEAS FROM
THE CITY'S FINEST CHEFS

A taste of
OXFORD

INSPIRED RECIPE IDEAS FROM
THE CITY'S FINEST CHEFS

First published 2004
by Midland Independent Magazines
Weaman Street, Birmingham B4 6AT

ISBN 0-9543388-2-0

Editor: Stacey Barnfield
Copy Editor: Louise Palfreyman
Product Manager: Anthony Bisseker
Main photography: Edward Moss
Additional photograhy: Craig Holmes
Production Manager: Julia Gregory

Printed by Butler & Tanner Group, Frome, Somerset.

A  Trinity Mirror business

FOOD ORDER

A taste of
OXFORD
INSPIRED RECIPE IDEAS FROM
THE CITY'S FINEST CHEFS

Photography by Edward Moss

Contents

ALL DISHES ARE BASED ON A SERVING OF FOUR, UNLESS OTHERWISE STATED.

FOREWORD

Oxford has to be one of the most beautiful cities in the world, with its spectacular architecture and streetscape. In many ways, it is a secret city with much of its beauty and interest located behind unprepossessing stone doorways which lead to College Quads which will simply take your breath away.

A guide will help you search out all the hidden gems and within easy walking distance are the famous colleges, punting on the the river, renowned gardens and museums, art galleries, the Covered Market and a multitude of interesting shops. Naturally, last but not least, you will find a truly amazing collection of well established and exciting restaurants and hotels.

Every cultural influence you can think of is reflected in our city's gastronomy, giving you the best of Britain, Italy, Lebanon, Thailand, France, Japan and India.

This excellent book provides you with a snapshot of all that Oxford has to offer with a tremendous collection of recipes. So, if you are preparing them yourself or decide to try the real thing by visiting us, I know you are going to enjoy great walking, great talking and fantastic eating.

Jeremy Mogford

Mogford Ltd

A taste of OXFORD

INSPIRED RECIPE IDEAS FROM
THE CITY'S FINEST CHEFS

YOUR TABLE IS READY...

BROOKES RESTAURANT

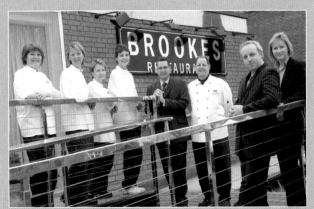

BROOKES RESTAURANT

When you come to Brookes Restaurant you'll soon discover why it has been awarded the 'Best Designed Restaurant and Bar' in the UK from GS Magazine's Hospitality Design Awards.

Our restaurant has become firmly established as one of the prime venues for dining in Oxford. Whether for a formal dinner party or a simple drinks reception, all you have to do is relax in our non-smoking environment and let our professional team take care of you in their characteristically friendly style.

We offer creative international cuisine and rely on the best quality ingredients, often sourced from local producers.

With such high standards it is easy to see why our hospitality management students gain so much from their experience of working in this unique restaurant. It's not surprising that so many of our customers come back time and time again.

Within easy reach of the city centre, Brookes Restaurant should be your next stop.

Brookes Restaurant team
www.brookes.ac.uk/restaurant

Salad of duck confit with pickled wild mushrooms and roast garlic dressing

INGREDIENTS

For the duck confit

5 duck legs

125g sea salt

1 carrot

1 onion

1/2 bunch thyme

6 bay leaves

500ml duck fat

For the pickled wild mushrooms

500g wild mushrooms

250g shallots

50ml olive oil

200ml tarragon vinegar

25ml Dijon mustard

50g sugar

100ml white wine

For the dressing

2 bulbs garlic

100ml olive oil

50ml white wine

To serve

1 small head radicchio lettuce

1 lollo rosso lettuce

1/2 bunch tarragon

30 small asparagus spears

METHOD

For the duck confit

Trim duck legs of excess fat and skin, place onto tray, sprinkle with salt, cover and leave for at least two hours in the refrigerator. Remove duck from tray and rinse and dry to get rid of excess salt. Preheat oven to 150°C.

Peel and dice the carrot and onion. Place duck in an ovenproof dish with the vegetables, thyme, bay leaves and melted duck fat, cover with a lid and cook for at least two hours or until the meat comes off the bone. When cold enough pick duck into pieces.

For the pickled wild mushrooms

Peel and finely slice shallots. Trim and wash mushrooms and place in oven to dry out.

Sweat shallots in a little oil, add the mustard, sugar and vinegar. Reduce gently and add the white wine and mushrooms then reduce once again until all the liquid has been absorbed.

For the dressing

Split garlic into cloves but do not peel, roast until soft in the middle. Keep back ten whole cloves for garnish then blend the rest with white wine and olive oil, pass through a chinois.

To serve

Trim and blanch asparagus, pick and wash lettuce. Arrange radicchio, lollo rosso and asparagus tips on a plate and randomly sprinkle with the duck and mushrooms. Top with a whole garlic clove, the dressing and tarragon leaves.

BROOKES RESTAURANT

Oxford Brookes University, Headington Campus, Gipsy Lane, Oxford OX3 0BP

Tel: 01865 483803

www.brookes.ac.uk/restaurant

Pan-fried red snapper on hot salad niçoise with carrot and star anise cream

INGREDIENTS

For the red snapper
6 x 200g red snapper

Seasoning to taste

100ml olive oil

For the purée
100g leeks

100g frozen peas

100g spinach

20g parsley (fresh)

50g butter

Seasoning to taste

For the cream
50g butter

250g carrots

500ml fish stock

2-3 star anise

1 stick celery

Pinch turmeric

200ml cream

1 lemon – juice and zest

Seasoning to taste

50ml white wine

For the hot salad niçoise
500g new potatoes

200g cherry tomatoes

200g green beans

200g spinach

20g black olives

Seasoning to taste

100ml olive oil

For garnish
1 carrot

METHOD

For the red snapper
Check fish for bones, trim, score and season well.

For the purée
Finely chop the leeks and wash well, wash spinach and defrost peas. Melt butter in a pan, add leeks and sweat for about 10 minutes until soft, add spinach, parsley and peas, heat gently for five minutes, season well. Purée in processor or liquidiser.

For the cream
Peel and roughly dice the carrots, wash and dice the celery. Put fish stock onto boil with star anise. Melt butter, add carrot and celery, sweat, add turmeric, lemon zest and white wine, reduce, add the stock and reduce until all the vegetables are tender. Liquidise and pass, add cream and lemon juice, boil and simmer, check seasoning and keep hot.

For the salad niçoise
Wash and cook potatoes in boiling salted water, refresh and cut to size required. Cut tomatoes in half. Trim beans and cook in boiling salted water, refresh. Pick, wash and drain spinach. Heat olive oil in pan, add potatoes to heat through then add spinach, beans, tomatoes and olives and toss to heat through and season.

For garnish
Peel the carrot and cut into long strips and deep-fry until crisp, drain and keep hot.

To serve
Brush fish with oil and pan-fry skin side down to achieve a golden brown colour and finish in oven. Serve fish on top of salad niçoise with vegetable purée, crisp carrot and surround with carrot sauce.

BROOKES RESTAURANT
Oxford Brookes University, Headington Campus, Gipsy Lane, Oxford OX3 0BP
Tel: 01865 483803
www.brookes.ac.uk/restaurant

Cardamon brûlée with lemongrass sorbet, tomato and lime syrup

INGREDIENTS

For the brûlée

350ml cream

110ml milk

8 egg yolks

56g caster sugar

6 cardamon pods crushed

For the sorbet

150ml stock syrup

2 lemons

1 stick lemon grass

For the tuile

125g flour

100g egg whites

125g butter

155g icing sugar

For the croquant

30g ground almonds

$1/_4$ tbsp glucose syrup

75g sugar

$1/_4$ orange – zest and juice

25g plain flour

25ml orange juice

50g melted butter

For the lime syrup

200g sugar

10ml water

1 lime – juice and zest

1tsp glucose syrup

1 tomato

METHOD

You will need an ice cream maker for this recipe.

For the brûlée

Crush cardamom pods, add to milk and cream, bring to the boil. Whisk together sugar and egg yolks, pour over milk and cream mix. Pass through a fine sieve and pour into moulds. Cook in a bain marie at 150°C until set (40 minutes). Chill.

For the sorbet

Bruise and chop lemon grass, zest and squeeze lemons. Bring stock syrup and lemon grass, zest and juice to the boil, allow to cool. Churn in ice cream machine and freeze.

For the tuile

Blend butter and icing sugar in a mixer until creamy, add egg white followed by the flour. Using a template spread on baking tray and bake at 180°C until golden brown.

For the croquant

Place all dry ingredients in a bowl. Melt butter with glucose syrup, add orange zest and juice, add to the dry mixture. Place a small amount on a greased baking try and cook in oven for two minutes until golden brown. While still hot shape around a rolling pin.

For the lime syrup

Place all ingredients in a pan, except tomato, boil until the sugar has dissolved and the mixture becomes syrupy. Skin, deseed and dice the tomato and add to the syrup.

To serve

Place brûlée and croquant on a dessert plate, Shape sorbet into quenelles place as required, decorate with tuile and dress plate with tomato stock syrup.

BROOKES RESTAURANT

Oxford Brookes University, Headington Campus, Gipsy Lane, Oxford OX3 0BP

Tel: 01865 483803

www.brookes.ac.uk/restaurant

BROWNS
RESTAURANT & BAR

Peter Alderin,
general manager

BROWNS RESTAURANT & BAR

Browns in Oxford opened in 1976, three years after the first restaurant in this now celebrated national collection.

A disused Morris garage was the location, and major building work transformed it into a restaurant and bar seating at first 160 people. Subsequent extensions have taken in an old ironmongery and electrical shop, increasing capacity to 230 covers.

With sister restaurants in Brighton, Cambridge, Bristol, Bath, Leeds, London and Edinburgh, Browns has been offering great food in beautiful locations for three decades. This makes it the longest established restaurant group in Britain, and Browns boasts some of the country's most experienced and creative chefs.

At Browns Oxford, you will find the magic formula that has created success all over the UK.

Browns is about people, and Denise Wheeler and head chef Ray Daykin are living proof of that, Denise has clocked up 20 years service as a host, and Ray has been with Browns for more than 10 years. Brought in to trial the concept, Denise proved so popular that her valued position has been replicated at all the restaurants.

You'll love the food at Browns, but it's the fun atmosphere, great cocktails, impressive wine list and that certain 'je ne sais quoi' that will really impress.

Caesar salad

1 cos lettuce, washed and dried

50g Parmesan cheese

8oz anchovy fillets

Caesar dressing

1 egg yolk

2 cloves garlic

1tsp powdered English mustard

Juice of one lemon

4 anchovies, chopped

Salt and pepper

3floz vegetable oil

2floz olive oil

2tbsp Parmesan cheese

2tbsp finely chopped fresh parsley

Croutons

1 clove garlic

2tbsp olive oil

1tbsp Parmesan cheese

6oz bread, cut into 1cm squares

2oz butter

Preheat the oven to 140ºC. To make the croutons, mix together the garlic, olive oil and butter in a large bowl. Toss the bread cubes in the mixture to coat then transfer to a baking sheet in a single layer.

Put in the oven for about 10 minutes, and check progress for next five minutes until crisp. Then cool.

For the dressing, put the egg yolk, garlic, mustard, lemon juice, anchovies and seasoning in a blender, or bowl, and blend for a few seconds before drizzling in the oils until smooth and thickened. Stir in the Parmesan cheese and parsley and refrigerate until needed.

Tear the lettuce into bite-sized pieces just before serving. Mix with the dressing, divide between serving bowls and top with a cross of anchovy fillets. Garnish with croutons and Parmesan shavings and serve.

BROWNS RESTAURANT & BAR
5-11 Woodstock Road, Oxford OX2 6HA
Tel: 01865 511995
www.browns-restaurants.com

Steak Guinness and mushroom pie

INGREDIENTS

500g braising steak, trimmed and cut into 2.5cm chunks	1tbsp Worcester sauce
4tbsp flour	100ml Guinness
45g onion, chopped	50ml red wine
45g carrot, chopped	1 bay leaf
45g celery, chopped	1tbsp tomato purée
225g button mushrooms	Salt and pepper
6tbsp olive oil	60g puff pastry shaped into lid
1tbsp sugar	Milk or beaten egg to glaze

METHOD

Heat 2tbsp oil in a pan and cook the onion until softened. Add the carrot, celery and mushrooms and cook for five minutes until the mushrooms are soft. Remove vegetables from pan and place in casserole.

Place flour on a plate and roll steak cubes until covered. Fry in batches in the pan until browned on all sides, adding more oil if necessary. Remove cooked steak to casserole with vegetables.

Add Guinness, red wine, bay leaf, tomato purée and seasoning to casserole and bring to boil. Reduce heat and cook on hob, simmering for two hours until tender, or cook at 170°C in oven for two hours. Check liquid level, topping up with a little water if necessary.

When cooked, place contents in wide baking dish and cool. Roll out pastry and cover baking dish, trimming off excess and sealing edges. Brush with milk or beaten egg and place in oven at 200°C for 30 minutes until pastry is golden and risen and pie heated through.

BROWNS RESTAURANT & BAR
5-11 Woodstock Road, Oxford OX2 6HA
Tel: 01865 511995
www.browns-restaurants.com

Sticky toffee pudding

INGREDIENTS

170g chopped dates

170g caster sugar

50g butter

1 egg

1tsp bicarbonate of soda

1tsp baking powder

1tsp vanilla essence

225g plain flour

300ml boiling water

Sauce

210g brown sugar

125g butter

130g whipping cream

METHOD

Preheat the oven to 180°C. Sift flour and baking powder together and put dates, bicarbonate of soda and vanilla in boiling water. Cream together butter and sugar, beat in egg, flour and baking powder.

When this mixture is firm, blend in the dates, soda and vanilla mixture. Pour into a buttered nine-inch square baking pan. Bake for 30-35 minutes until firm to the touch. Meanwhile, place all of the sauce ingredients into a pan and melt slowly then boil for one minute. When the pudding is removed from the oven, pour some of the sauce over the top and place in the oven until it bubbles. Serve the pudding with the remainder of the sauce.

BROWNS RESTAURANT & BAR
5-11 Woodstock Road, Oxford OX2 6HA
Tel: 01865 511995
www.browns-restaurants.com

THE DEDDINGTON ARMS

Head chef Paul Haverson

THE DEDDINGTON ARMS

The Deddington Arms Restaurant overlooks the beautiful market square of Deddington, a medieval village lying between Oxford and Banbury at the gateway to the Cotswolds.

The Deddington Arms began as a coaching inn in the 16th Century when it offered food and shelter to weary stagecoach passengers. Today it enjoys an outstanding reputation for serving superb modern English food in a friendly and efficient atmosphere and prides itself on being the only restaurant in the Banbury area to be awarded an AA Rosette. The interior of the Deddington Arms Restaurant has been recently refurbished and the introduction of air-conditioning ensures you can eat in comfort whatever the season. Private dinner parties of up to 16 diners are welcomed in a separate room with your choice of menu, wines, and music!

Head chef Paul Haverson has designed a menu to appeal to lovers of fresh food cooked simply but with subtle variations in taste and texture. Fresh fish dishes and vegetarian options are always available and the menu is supported by a good quality wine list featuring wines from around the world.

The Deddington Arms Restaurant hosts many special events throughout the year as well as unique à la carte weekend breaks including accommodation at the Deddington Arms Hotel to allow you to fully enjoy the very best of fine cuisine.

Pigeon and bacon salad

INGREDIENTS

8 pigeon breasts

Fresh rosemary, garlic, olive oil – for marinade

8 bacon rashers

1 red apple

1 green apple

Mixed salad leaves

500ml water

500g sugar

Port wine glaze

125g redcurrant jelly

3floz ruby port

Juice of 1 lemon

Juice of 1 orange

$1/_2$ cinnamon stick

$1/_2$tsp English mustard

METHOD

Marinade pigeon breasts in rosemary, garlic and olive oil for four hours in fridge.

Cook the rashers of bacon and leave to the side.

Core the apples leaving them whole and then slice thinly.

Make simple stock syrup with water and sugar, bring to the boil and simmer for five minutes. Place apple in syrup, take off heat and leave until syrup has cooled.

Slice bacon into strips.

Port wine glaze

Place all ingredients in saucepan. Bring to boil and reduce over a low heat for approximately 15-20 minutes. Strain through a fine sieve and cool.

To serve

Pan fry pigeon breasts on both sides and place in oven and cook at 160ºC for 3-4 minutes.

While pigeon is cooking dress mixed leaves in olive oil and place bacon strips in oven to warm through.

Place leaves in middle of plate and alternate strips of bacon and apple on leaves.

Slice cooked pigeon breasts in half and place on leaves, then spoon port wine glaze around plate.

THE DEDDINGTON ARMS
Horsefair, Deddington, Oxfordshire OX15 OSH
Tel: 01869 338364
www.deddington-arms-hotel.co.uk

Fillet of monkfish served with an orange butter sauce

INGREDIENTS

1kg monkfish tail	200ml orange juice
2 courgettes	125g unsalted butter
2 carrots	100ml double cream
1 packet Thai asparagus	Salmon keta
4 rashers smoked bacon	Chervil
20 turned new potatoes	

METHOD

Cut monkfish into four pieces. Wrap smoked bacon around each piece of monkfish and season. Place fish in oven to cook at 170°C for 15-20 minutes.

Place orange juice in pan and reduce by half. Add cream then reduce again by half and add unsalted butter in small amounts until all is melted keeping pan on the move. Season.

Peel carrots and use a potato peeler to make long strips of courgette and carrot. Blanche Thai asparagus in hot salted water for 40 seconds so it is still crisp.

Turn new potatoes with a paring knife into barrel shapes and cook in salted boiling water.

To serve

Place courgette and carrot ribbons in boiling water for 15 seconds. Take out of water and place in the centre of plate.

Slice monkfish and place in a circle onto the carrot and courgette. Place warmed asparagus in middle of monkfish standing upwards.

Spoon butter sauce around dish and place hot new potatoes at three points around plate.

Place salmon keta in between potatoes and garnish with chervil.

THE DEDDINGTON ARMS

Horsefair, Deddington, Oxfordshire OX15 OSH
Tel: 01869 338364
www.deddington-arms-hotel.co.uk

Citron tart with elderflower sorbet

1 sweet pastry case 10 inch (bought)

Lemon tart filling

7 eggs

3 egg yolks

340g caster sugar

Juice of 7 lemons

Juice of 3 oranges

460ml double cream

Elderflower sorbet

375g caster sugar, for syrup

375ml water, for syrup

2tbsp elderflower cordial

250ml water

Juice of 3 lemons

Tuille biscuits

45g unsalted butter

250g caster sugar

45g plain flour

Whites of 5 eggs

Zest of 1 orange

To serve

Passion fruit coulis to serve (bought and boiled with 75g sugar to sweeten)

Raspberries

Icing sugar

You will need an ice-cream maker for this recipe.

Lemon tart filling

Whisk the eggs, egg yolk and sugar together by hand. Juice oranges and lemons and place in saucepan with cream and bring to boil.

Mix cream and juices into egg mixture. Place pastry case in oven and taking the lemon mixture to the oven, pour it into the case and fill to the top, being careful not to spill any. It is easier to do this at the oven, rather than on the worktop.

Bake at 120°C for 45-50 minutes until set, remove, cool and refrigerate.

Elderflower sorbet

Make the syrup by boiling up sugar and water. Leave for five minutes to cool. Add rest of ingredients and place in ice-cream maker and churn.

Tuille biscuits

Melt butter in pan over low heat. Mix caster sugar and flour in bowl, add egg whites, melted butter and orange zest, mix to smooth paste. Rest for two hours. Heat oven to 160°C and spread onto buttered baking sheet, making eight inch strips.

Work in batches of four at a time and bake each batch for 10 minutes until pale brown. Immediately wrap strips around a 3.5inch (9cms) pastry cutter (not too tightly) and leave to harden slightly before gently removing.

To serve

Cut portions of tart and sprinkle with icing sugar. Glaze with blowtorch. Put passion fruit coulis on centre of plate and place tart on top. Place tuille ring next to tart and place sorbet in centre, garnishing with raspberries and a sprinkling of icing sugar.

THE DEDDINGTON ARMS

Horsefair, Deddington, Oxfordshire OX15 OSH

Tel: 01869 338364

www.deddington-arms-hotel.co.uk

THE EAGLE TAVERN

THE EAGLE TAVERN

The Eagle Tavern in Little Coxwell was built in 1901 as a pub to serve the local farming community. Set in the beautiful Vale of the White Horse, the tavern has seen many changes, both in its clientele and style of service. The pub was remodelled in the 1990s by its then owner Mark Lawrenson, the Ireland international footballer.

The last change was the creation of Chester's Restaurant. The vision was to create a fine dining experience that would work in harmony with the traditional trade of the tavern. The restaurant has its own identity and has a light and airy feel for formal or informal lunches but transforms into a very intimate, classic yet contemporary restaurant after dark. The ambience is friendly and relaxed, but with an air of formality.

Chester's Restaurant menus are based on classic European cuisine and imaginatively incorporate flavours and ideas from around the world. The focus is on maximising the flavours of the ingredients and presenting them beautifully. We work hard to source local supplies of the highest quality, and it shows.

The menu offers excellent variety and is changed frequently according to the season and the careful selection of only the best available produce. Our splendid food is complemented by a carefully chosen and varied list of well priced wines.

In short, Chester's offers a relaxing gastronomic experience for any occasion, where you can be sure of a warm welcome and attention to detail. We look forward to seeing you.

Rachel Baker

Timbale of shellfish

INGREDIENTS

4tbsp crème fraîche

4 slices smoked salmon

1lb white crab meat

2 ripe avocados

8oz fresh prawns

2 fresh peeled mangos, sliced and diced

4 tomatoes, concassé

4 queen scallops

Handful chervil

Pinch of curry powder

Vinaigrette

14floz extra virgin olive oil

6 leaves of basil diced and bruised

14floz groundnut oil

1oz finely grated ginger

$1/_2$tsp fine sea salt (half a teaspoon)

$1/_2$tsp ground black pepper

juice of two limes

$3^1/_2$floz white wine vinegar

$3^1/_2$floz sherry vinegar

METHOD

Mix flaked crab meat with seasoning, crème fraîche and curry powder and set to one side. Place four two-inch cutting rings into the centre of four white plates and place diced fresh mango in base, spread this smooth with the back of a spoon. Next put a layer of avocado onto the mango, lay prawns on the avocado then tomato concassé on the prawns and then another of mango. Use the crab mixture as the final layer. Cut four two-inch rounds of smoked salmon and place this on top. Whisk together vinaigrette ingredients together and drizzle around the edge of the plate using a teaspoon.

Season the scallops with a little salt and pepper and dust with curry powder. Heat one tablespoon of oil in a pan and when hot add the scallops and cook each side for a minute. Remove from the pan and toss in some of the vinaigrette.

Gently ease the cutting ring from the timbale. Place the scallop on top of the timbale and garnish with chervil.

THE EAGLE TAVERN
Little Coxwell, Faringdon, Oxfordshire SN7 7LW
Tel: 01367 240120
www.eagletavern.co.uk

Tournedos rossinni

INGREDIENTS

4 x 8oz prime fillet steaks

4 slices brioche

12 girolle mushrooms

Pinch salt and pepper

Handful parsley

Olive oil

Liver paté

20oz chicken liver

$2^1/_2$floz brandy

Pinch of salt and pepper

8floz double cream

Madeira sauce

2oz Spanish onions finely diced

4oz chestnut mushrooms

1oz fresh tarragon

1oz chopped parsley

$^1/_4$pt Madeira

$^1/_4$pt beef stock

METHOD

Liver paté

Fry chicken livers in a little olive oil in a hot frying pan for four or five minutes. Remove livers and place in blender with brandy, cream and seasoning and blend until smooth. Form into four two-inch squares and refrigerate.

Season the fillet steaks and fry in a little olive oil quickly on each side to seal and brown. Place on a tray and place in the oven at 200ºC. Keep juices from the steak pan for the Madeira sauce. Gently fry onions and chestnut mushrooms. Add beef stock and Madeira.

Reduce by half and add parsley and tarragon. Pass through a strainer. Cut a two-inch round slice of brioche and lightly toast each side. Place toast in the centre of a pasta bowl and place the fillet steak on top. Top the fillet with a square of paté. Garnish with three girolle mushrooms per steak that have been lightly sautéed in butter and a sprig of parsley.

If you are up to it a tomato rose looks great!

THE EAGLE TAVERN
Little Coxwell, Faringdon, Oxfordshire SN7 7LW
Tel: 01367 240120
www.eagletavern.co.uk

Chocolate Bavarois on white chocolate brownies

White chocolate brownie

1tsp baking powder

1tsp salt

6 large eggs

3oz sugar

1tbsp vanilla

10oz white chocolate

6oz white unsalted butter

10oz unbleached all purpose flour

16 prunes soaked in Armagnac to serve

Bavarois

$3/_4$pt milk

2 leaves gelatine

$2^1/_2$oz unsweetened dark chocolate

3oz castor sugar

2tsp vanilla

$1/_2$pt double cream

Coulis

4 passion fruits

2oz sugar

$2^1/_2$floz Campari

White chocolate brownie

Pre-heat oven to 185°C. Line a 9x2 inch tin with foil. Butter the foil.

Reserve a third of the white chocolate. Combine remaining chocolate with butter in a small saucepan over a low heat. When fully melted stir in flour, baking powder and salt. Using a mixer beat eggs, sugar and vanilla until fluffy. Stir in chocolate mixture, then fold in the remaining dry ingredients. Spread mixture into tin and bake for 45 minutes. Cool in the tin on a rack.

Bavarois

Put milk in a pan sprinkle in gelatine and soften. Add chocolate and sugar and cook over a medium heat until chocolate melts. Leave to cool until just warm, then add vanilla. Whip the cream and then fold this into the chocolate mixture.

Passion fruit and Campari coulis

Halve two of the passion fruit and scoop the pulp into a bowl add the sugar and the Campari and whiz in a blender.

To assemble

For each serving cut out a round of brownie with a two-inch cutter, leaving the brownie in the cutter and place on top of four prunes that have been soaked in Armagnac. Pour in chocolate mixture and refrigerate. Transfer set Bavarois onto a dessert plate and drizzle coulis around the mousse. Garnish with scrolls of white chocolate and passion fruit flowers.

THE EAGLE TAVERN

Little Coxwell, Faringdon, Oxfordshire SN7 7LW
Tel: 01367 240120
www.eagletavern.co.uk

FISHERS

*Simone Taylor,
manager*

FISHERS

Fishers opened in 1995 and is now established as Oxford's premier fish and seafood restaurant.

We choose, prepare, cook and serve fresh fish and shellfish, which according to some would be a difficult task, as Oxford is far from the sea.

We decided to set up a small fish carriage company to enable us to buy direct from fishermen and markets up and down the country for our daily changing menu.

There are frequent phone calls to and fro to discuss weather conditions, catches, and market availability and even now there is still excitement opening the ice-packed delivery boxes to find either glistening black rope grown mussels from the Highlands of Scotland, wonderfully fresh turbot from Wales, or Cornish red mullet that have come in on the day boats.

At Fishers we enjoy keeping the dishes simple, and use only the freshest seasonal produce.

Our menu has something for everyone; from grilled Canadian lobsters, to hot shellfish platters, where the base of mussels, cockles and langoustines is poached with white wine garlic and cream, topped with grilled scallops and prawns, to the best beer battered traditional haddock and chips with tartare sauce.

Oxford has an eclectic mix of people including dons, professors, students, visiting celebrities and local residents and with Fishers' friendly and informal atmosphere we create a fun place to eat and drink in the company of colleagues, friends and family.

Martin Agius, Angie Parmenter, James Jasper, Stephane Chamusard

www.fishers-restaurant.com

Grilled king scallops with ginger, soy, garlic, chilli and coriander with toasted sesame seeds

INGREDIENTS

12 hand-dived King scallops

2tsp chopped ginger

1tsp chopped garlic

1tsp chopped shallots

1 chopped red chilli

1dsp sugar

1dsp soy sauce

1dsp red wine vinegar

5dsp sesame oil

1dsp toasted sesame seeds

2-3dsp chopped coriander

METHOD

Put the chopped shallots, ginger, garlic, together with the sugar in a pestle and mortar and mince finely.

Mix the soy sauce, red wine vinegar and sesame oil together and add the minced ingredients.

Chop the chilli and coriander and toast the sesame seeds, mix together and reserve for the topping.

Rinse the scallops under gently running water and keep some of the shells for serving.

Pat dry with kitchen paper and quickly pan fry the scallops in a little olive oil until golden on one side.

Assemble the scallops in the shells and drizzle the dressing over them. Flash them under the grill for one minute and then sprinkle the sesame seeds, coriander and chilli mix over the top and serve.

FISHERS

36/37 St Clements, Oxford OX4 1AB
Tel: 01865 243003
www.fishers-restaurant.com

Roasted fillets of royal sea bream (gilthead) on celeriac mash with a red chilli and coriander butter

INGREDIENTS

For the sea bream

4 large sea bream (eight fillets; you could ask your fishmonger to fillet them and keep the bones for the fish stock)

50g plain flour

Olive oil

Salt and pepper

For the mash

500g celeriac

200g potato

Juice of $^1/_2$ lemon

30g butter

For the sauce

30g red chilli

1 dsp fresh coriander, finely chopped

1 dsp fresh lemon grass, finely chopped

60g butter

10cl white wine

10cl fish stock

1 dsp shallots, finely chopped

METHOD

For the celeriac mash

Chop the celeriac and potato into similar sized pieces and cook in boiling water with half the lemon juice for around 15 minutes or until soft.

Drain and mash them adding 30g of butter and salt and pepper to taste.

For the sea bream

Flour and season the fillets on both sides.

Heat some olive oil in a pan and fry both sides of the fillets until light brown in colour.

Finish them in a preheated oven at 180°C for 5-10 minutes depending on the size of the bream.

For the sauce

In a small pan, melt 10g of butter, add shallots and lemon grass and gently cook for one minute before adding the chilli and white wine.

Reduce for a few minutes.

Add 10cl of fish stock made with the fish bones to the rest of the lemon juice and coriander and reduce again until sauce consistency.

Finally, slowly whisk in the remainder of the cold butter.

To serve

Position the celeriac mash in the centre of the plate and place the sea bream on top. Pour the sauce around the plate and a little over the fish and garnish.

FISHERS

36/37 St Clements, Oxford OX4 1AB
Tel: 01865 243003
www.fishers-restaurant.com

Poached figs in red wine with mascarpone

INGREDIENTS

12 fresh figs

75cl red wine

300g sugar

3 star anise

1 cinnamon stick

250g mascarpone

Mint and redcurrants to garnish

METHOD

Pour the red wine into a heavy-bottomed pan, add star anise, cinnamon stick and the sugar, then add the figs

Bring to the boil and turn off immediately, let it rest for about 15 minutes until the figs are cooked through.

Remove the figs and allow to cool. Reduce the remaining liquid until it becomes syrupy.

Cut the figs in half and fill with the mascarpone.

Arrange on a plate and pour over some red wine syrup add a sprig of mint and a small bunch of redcurrants and dust with some icing sugar.

FISHERS
36/37 St Clements, Oxford OX4 1AB
Tel: 01865 243003
www.fishers-restaurant.com

GEE'S

The Gee's team

GEE'S

Formally a florist and greengrocers, Gee's, a Victorian conservatory now houses an elegant restaurant and bar with a collection of Gary Hume's artwork.

Comfortable banquettes surround the restaurant's perimeter with tables dressed in white linen, an elegant though unpretentious space and glamorous pit stop for pre- and post-theatre diners. Food focuses on modern British with the emphasis on quality seasonal produce. Head chef Michael Wright leads a team of ten chefs who combine age and experience with youth and enthusiasm. Their philosophy, to source the best possible ingredients and support local and regional suppliers. Beef from Buccleuch Estate, traditional cured bacon from Wiltshire, Durrock Pork from Suffolk, fish and shellfish direct from Jersey and local cheese such as Isis and Oxford Blue are all regulars on the menu.

Jazz at Gee's every Sunday night has become an institution in Oxford as has 'British Weekend Brunch' available every Saturday and Sunday from 11.00am.

The young, cosmopolitan staff who double as poets, philosophers and artists are well-drilled, having a broad knowledge of the menu and wine list and importing quality yet unobtrusive service.

Gee's is a five minute bus ride from Oxford city centre in North Oxford, and has been featured in the Good Food Guide 2003/2004, AA The Restaurant Guide, Harpers and Queen Restaurant Guide 2004, Observer 500 Best Restaurants 2003.

Marie Jackson, general manager

King scallops with green beans, leeks and shallot dressing

INGREDIENTS

400g green beans, cooked

12 king scallops

2 leeks, washed

4 shallots

4tbsp balsamic vinegar

7tbsp extra virgin olive oil

60g butter

Salt and pepper

METHOD

Soak finely diced shallots in vinegar and six tablespoons of olive oil.

Pour remaining oil over scallops.

Place in a hot non-stick pan and cook approximately 30 seconds each side. Season with salt and pepper.

In another pan cook the leeks gently in the butter and add the green beans and warm through.

Divide leeks and beans between plates, add scallops and pour over shallot dressing.

GEE'S

61 Banbury Road, Oxford OX2 6NN

Tel: 01865 553540

www.oxford-hotels-restaurants.co.uk

Pan-fried veal chop with chips, red wine mustard and rosemary vinaigrette

INGREDIENTS

4 x 400g veal chops

2kg Desiree red potatoes

Red wine mustard or a good quality grain mustard

250ml beef stock

250ml olive oil

2 sprigs rosemary

Red wine mustard

1kg mustard seeds

1.2 litre red wine

1.6 litre red wine vinegar

1.2 litre water

250g honey

1tbsp allspice berries

1tbsp black pepper

Sea salt

Garlic purée

METHOD

Cut potatoes into chips and cook in oil at 130°C until tender, strain and set aside.

Rosemary vinaigrette

Mix the olive oil with the beef stock and heat with two sprigs of rosemary for 30 minutes, then strain.

Red wine mustard

Soak mustard seeds with the wine vinegar, 1.2 litres of the water, the honey and the allspice berries, seasoning and garlic purée. Leave for 24 hours. Liquidise and cook gently for six hours.

Cook veal in a non-stick frying pan for about six to eight minutes on each side and let rest for six minutes.

Re-fry chips at 170°C, strain, add salt and share between plates. Place veal on top and add mustard and vinaigrette.

GEE'S
61 Banbury Road, Oxford OX2 6NN
Tel: 01865 553540
www.oxford-hotels-restaurants.co.uk

Steamed marmalade sponge pudding

INGREDIENTS

Marmalade

3 lemons

3 oranges

4 pints water

1200g caster sugar

Custard or clotted cream

Sponge

80g butter

200g suet (vegetable)

360g plain flour

360g breadcrumbs

25g bicarbonate of soda

600ml milk

225g caster sugar

METHOD

Marmalade

Segment the flesh and peel the zest from fruit and cut thinly. Cover with water, heat slowly for one-two hours. Add sugar and simmer for 20 to 30 minutes. (Any over can be stored in a preserving jar).

Mix all ingredients together. Place a tablespoon of marmalade in greased dariole moulds and fill up with sponge mixture.

Place in a bain marie, cover and cook at 180°C for one hour.

Turn out and pour over custard or clotted cream.

Makes approximately eight sponges.

GEE'S

61 Banbury Road, Oxford OX2 6NN

Tel: 01865 553540

www.oxford-hotels-restaurants.co.uk

HAWKWELL HOUSE HOTEL

HAWKWELL HOUSE HOTEL

Hawkwell House is a quintessentially English country hotel set within three acres of well-designed mature tree-lined gardens.

The Georgian-style 66 bed hotel used to be a private residence, and on arrival you will notice at once a sense of calm... a tranquil oasis.

The hotel is in the leafy village of Iffley on the River Thames, near the centre of Oxford, and diners and guests alike enjoy the ambiance of a traditional English countryside setting.

Hawkwell House Hotel is owned by Furlong Hotels, the same people behind the world-famous Lygon Arms in the Cotswolds village of Broadway.

Excellent service, sumptuous décor, fine dining and attention to detail are therefore assured.

Arezzo is the award-winning restaurant that forms the heart of Hawkwell House Hotel – an Italian feel pervades with conservatory, marble floor and a light and airy aspect overlooking a stunning patio with fountain.

Head chef Laurent Guyon produces fine modern Italian dishes using fresh ingredients and produce. Bread is made on site and a fine wine list accompanies the menu.

Arezzo boasts an AA rosett and the menu changes every six weeks in line with the seasons. So whether it's a light meal of, for example, Mediterranean fish soup and spinach and ricotta tortellini, or the richer offering of duck liver parfait and succulent Scotch rib-eye steak, you are sure to enjoy your dining experience with us.

Hawkwell House Hotel
www.hawkwellhouse.co.uk

Quail tartelette with celeriac purée, wild mushroom and port sauce

INGREDIENTS

4 quail

4 quail eggs (poached)

250g celeriac purée

100g spinach

100g trompette de la mont (wild mushrooms)

4 shortcrust pasty tartlets

1 tomato, concasse

Sauce

2 shallots, finely chopped

20ml serving port

200ml quail stock

20ml strong red wine

1tsp white truffle oil

10g unsalted butter

METHOD

Pan-fry the quails until brown all over, then bake them in the oven for seven minutes at 180°C.

While the quails are cooking, reheat the celeriac purée in a small saucepan. In a different saucepan, fry the spinach and the wild mushrooms for a couple of minutes.

Remove the quails and drain the fat, then add the shallots to the quail pan. Deglaze first with the port, then add the red wine and reduce down to a syrup consistency.

Warm the tartlets in the oven.

Now add the quail stock and pass it through a fine sieve. Add the butter, wild mushrooms and tomato concasse.

To serve

Place warmed tartlet in the middle of plate, spoon some of the spinach into the tartlet, place a quail on top.

Place three quenelles of celeriac purée and spoon the sauce between, then position quail eqqs.

Drizzle a few drops of truffle oil onto the purée surrounding the tartlet to garnish.

HAWKWELL HOUSE HOTEL
Church Way, Iffley Village, Oxford OX4 4DZ
Tel: 01865 749988
www.hawkwellhouse.co.uk

Fillet of beef with pommes boulangère, plum tomato, braised white onion and Bordelaise sauce

INGREDIENTS

4 x 180g fillets of beef

4 large King Edward potatoes

6 large plum tomatoes, peeled

2 large white onions

100g beef marrow (diced and poached)

1 branch of thyme

Olive oil

10g butter

Pinch of sea salt

Sauce

500ml of beef stock

2 shallots

1 bay leaf

1 bottle strong good quality red wine

500ml of white chicken stock

1 litre of dry white wine

Cracked black pepper

METHOD

Slice the white onion and cook in a large pan until soft, but do not burn or discolour. Deglaze with white wine and reduce. Add some of your chicken stock, cover and cook slowly in the oven for 45 minutes at 120°C.

Whilst the above is cooking, slice the potatoes into 3mm slices and shape with a pastry cutter with a diameter of 3cm. Place in a saucepan and cover with some of the chicken stock, fresh thyme and butter, cook slowly on a low heat. Slice tomatoes.

Sauce

Peel and chop the shallots and cook in a large saucepan until soft. Add the pepper, bayleaf and thyme, deglaze with half the red wine and bring it to the boil, once boiling set alight, then reduce down to a glace. Add this to the beef stock and keep heated on a low setting for 30 minutes, then strain.

Using another saucepan, reduce down the half of the red wine down to glace, then mix it all in with the above.

Pan fry the beef until cooked to your liking.

To serve

Reheat the tomatoes in olive oil, then place on a plate. Arrange in a circle of braised onion, tomato and potatoes. Place the beef fillet on top and pour the sauce around the above.

HAWKWELL HOUSE HOTEL
Church Way, Iffley Village, Oxford OX4 4DZ
Tel: 01865 749988
www.hawkwellhouse.co.uk

Croustillant of fresh fruit, green apple mousse and clementine sorbet served with Suzette sauce

Orange brandy snap
250g sugar
75g plain flour
10cl orange juice
125g melted butter
Zest of half an orange

Suzette sauce
Zest and juice of 1
orange
60g butter
30ml Grand Marnier
60g sugar

Clementine sorbet
500g of clementines
60g sugar
20g glucose
1tbsp water

Green apple mousse
3cl stock syrup
3cl apple purée
(Granny Smith)
Few drops lemon juice
6cl whipped cream

Compote of citrus
2 grapefruits
1 orange
2 clementines
2g pectine

Garnish
1 punnet raspberries
1 punnet blueberries
$1/_2$ pineapple
1 kiwi fruit
100g sweet pastry

You will need a sorbet machine for this recipe.

Roll out sweet pastry to 5mm thick and cut into discs, 5cm in diameter and cook in the oven for 15 minutes at 180ºC.

Orange brandy snap
Melt the butter, mix all the ingredients in to the butter and let it cool down, then chill until ready to use. Spread walnut sized portions shaped into discs on two non-stick baking sheets (two discs per sheet) and bake at 180ºC for 10 minutes. When ready, cut to size and shape around a plastic cylinder or base of pudding bowl, and leave to cool.

Suzette sauce
Mix all the ingredients together in a saucepan and boil down to a syrup consistency.

Clementine sorbet
Heat up the sugar, water and glucose to make a syrup. Cool it down to 4ºC and add the clementines, puréed. Pour all ingredients into a sorbet machine and blend for approximately 10 minutes or until a smooth sorbet consistency appears.

Green apple mousse
Whip the cream, add the apple purée to the stock syrup and mix with lemon juice drops.

Compote of citrus
Segment all the fruit, keep all the juices that run from the fruit. Then cut the fruit into cubes, reduce the juices down in a saucepan and add the pectine. Mix fruit together and keep in the fridge until ready.

To serve
Seat the brandy snap on the sweet pastry biscuit, fill a third with green apple mousse, then a third with citrus compote and then fill the remaining space with the fresh fruit and sorbet as shown in the picture. Arrange a few fresh fruit on top and a few around the plate for presentation. Dot Suzette sauce around the brandy snap as shown in the picture.

HAWKWELL HOUSE HOTEL
Church Way, Iffley Village, Oxford OX4 4DZ
Tel: 01865 749988
www.hawkwellhouse.co.uk

THE KAZBAR

Chef Fez and Craig Morton, manager

THE KAZBAR

Situated on Oxford's liveliest stretch of the Cowley Road, the Kazbar is one of the best tapas bars you'll come across outside of Spain. The souk-inspired cavern, with sliding roof and courtyard, is ideal for a chilled out lunch or party night out.

It's full of Moroccan soul and accessories – big, comfy cushioned alcoves, mosaic tiled tables and gorgeous ornate lanterns.

The tapas are unashamedly delicious and start at around £2.50 each. You can mix and match to your heart's content. Try patatas con chorizo, chicken tagine, merguez sausage, mint and garlic infused cous cous and creamy houmous.

All are served with warm home baked bread. There's also a connoisseur's choice of sherries, (Jerez – served chilled to wonderful perfection), wines and beers as well as a small but well chosen list of home-grown cocktails.

The music is spot on and the service even better. It's no surprise that, despite recently doubling in size. The Kazbar is still one of Oxford's most popular eating and drinking holes – the hippy trail on your doorstep.

Recommended by The Times, Observer, Guardian Guide, Wine Magazine.

'*Funky, flavour-full tapas bar with Moorish leaning.*' The Times

'*The Kazbar can inject sunshine into your day, even if the weather outside isn't warming.*' Wine Magazine

Albóndigas
Kazbar beef meatballs with sherry sauce

INGREDIENTS

For the meatballs

500g best beef mince (10 per cent fat)

½ head of roasted garlic

1 finely diced chilli (or more to taste)

10ml Worcestershire sauce

10ml Tabasco sauce

100ml red wine

2 free range eggs

Handful of breadcrumbs

For the sauce

1 finely diced Spanish onion

50g plain flour

60g smoked Spanish paprika (could substitute with Hungarian paprika)

100ml dry sherry

500ml vegetable stock

400g tin of chopped tomatoes

50ml olive oil

For the meatballs

In a bowl, mix together thoroughly all the ingredients, but keep back half the bread crumbs. The consistency should be moist not wet. Add more of the breadcrumbs or a dash more wine as necessary. In your hands, roll the mix into walnut sized balls. Roast on a medium heat until browned, yet still a little pink in the middle. Remove from the oven to rest.

For the sauce

Sauté the onions in the olive oil until translucent, add the paprika and flour and cook on a low heat, stirring constantly for five minutes. While still stirring, (to avoid lumpy sauce) slowly add the stock, then tomatoes and finally sherry. Bring the sauce to a low simmer, reduce heat and cook for a further 10 minutes. Return the meatballs to the sauce and season to taste. Serve in a bowl with a few diced roasted Mediterranean vegetables and a sprinkle of fresh parsley.

Ibikha

2 butternut squash

Olive oil

1 Spanish onion

500g cooked chickpeas

1 400g tin chopped tomatoes

Handful of chopped fresh coriander

1tsp of harissa (North African chilli sauce)

Skin and chop the squash into 2cm cubes.

Sauté the onions in oil until translucent, add the squash and continue to cook for a further five minutes.

Add the chickpeas, tomatoes and harissa, cook for a further 10 minutes.

Season and add the chopped coriander.

THE KAZBAR
Cowley Road, Oxford OX4 1HP
Tel: 01865 202920

Albóndigas

Chicken tagine

8 free-range chicken legs

1 Spanish onion, roughly chopped

$1/2$ head of roasted garlic

1 preserved lemon (finely sliced)

1 litre of chicken stock

50g ginger

50g paprika

50g cumin

50g turmeric

10g ras el hanout (Moroccan spice blend)

20g sultanas

Handful of fresh roughly chopped coriander to finish

Traditionally cooked and served from a Moroccan clay tagine. It can however be prepared in a heavy based pan.

Marinate the chicken in the spices overnight.

Place all the ingredients in a pot and bring to the boil, reduce the heat and simmer for 20 minutes. Remove the chicken from the stock and continue to simmer until the liquor has reduced by half. Return the chicken to pan and warm through. Season to taste. To serve, sprinkle with the fresh coriander.

Cordero romero

500g diced lamb

1 onion, finely sliced

50g sun dried tomatoes

1 large sprig of rosemary, de-stalked and roughly chopped

4 cloves of garlic

400g cooked borlotti beans

125ml of manzanilla (dry sherry)

Juice of 2 lemons

1 finely sliced preserved orange

500ml lamb stock

Handful of fresh roughly chopped flat leafed parsley (to finish)

Marinate the lamb with the sun dried tomatoes, garlic, rosemary and lemon juice for 24 hours.

Brown the lamb in a pan add the onion, sauté until translucent.

Add the stock, preserved orange and sherry and simmer until the lamb is tender about 45 minutes to 1 hour.

Season to taste. To serve, sprinkle with fresh parsley.

THE KAZBAR
Cowley Road, Oxford OX4 1HP
Tel: 01865 202920

Figs with vanilla crème fraiche

INGREDIENTS

8 fresh, ripe figs

250g crème fraiche

1 vanilla pod

100g caster sugar

Zest of a lemon

METHOD

Add the caster sugar to 50ml of warm water, heat through to form a syrup. Add the lemon zest and the seeds from the vanilla pod, leave the syrup to stand for half an hour. Mix the syrup together with the crème fraiche. Serve with the sliced figs.

Manchego con membrillo

Manchego is a hard sheep's milk cheese from La Mancha in central Spain.

INGREDIENTS

For the marinade

A few sprigs of fresh thyme

A few cloves of finely sliced garlic

A good pinch of finely sliced chillies (to taste)

METHOD

Prepare several days in advance.

Marinate slices of Manchego in the oil for at least three days. Serve with membrillo (quince jelly), crusty bread and a glass of Oloroso sherry.

THE KAZBAR
Cowley Road, Oxford OX4 1HP
Tel: 01865 202920

THE LEMON TREE

THE LEMON TREE

Widely recognised as one of Oxford's best restaurants, The Lemon Tree is a must for diners seeking great food in an amazing location.

The striking Mediterranean inspired spacious interior creates a superb ambiance – bright and sunny by day and warm and intimate at night.

The menu offers a wide choice of classic and surprising treats. Starters include Torbay scallops exquisitely flavoured with lemon and herb butter, the finest black pudding from Clonakilty served with spring onion mash and a mustard dressing, and steamed mussels with saffron and chilli.

Mains include haddock topped with a poached egg and hollandaise sauce with mashed potatoes and minted peas, locally reared Charolais beef, and succulent slow cooked shank of lamb with rosemary and garlic served with a butternut squash risotto and a mint purée. Puds cater for all predilections, from a 'to die for' part-baked chocolate pudding to a pineapple tart tatin – a sumptuous twist to an old favourite. And, of course, there's an excellent selection of wines.

It's no wonder The Lemon Tree is frequented by the county's celebrity set. The unpretentious, superb service and reasonable prices, however, appeal to us all.

Open for dinner every night and all day for lunch Friday, Saturday and all day Sunday.

'*The best restaurant in Oxford by a long chalk.*' The Observer

'*It was absolutely delicious... the puddings were irresistible... an excellent evening.*' Waitrose Food Illustrated

The Lemon Tree

Torbay scallops with lemon and herb butter

12 scallops, opened, deskirted and cleaned, still attached to shell

12 slices lemon and herb butter

Lemon and herb butter

1 pack good quality unsalted butter, softened

1 handful finely chopped mixed herbs

– chervil, basil, parsley, chives

2 shallots, finely chopped

2 cloves garlic, finely chopped

1 tomato, deseeded, skinned and diced

Juice and zest of 1 unwaxed lemon

Salt and pepper

Lemon and herb butter

Beat all the ingredients together using a whisk or wooden spoon and roll into a sausage shape. Wrap in clingfilm or greaseproof paper. Chill to set. Any leftover butter can be frozen for up to one month.

Brush the scallops with a little olive oil or butter and place under a hot grill for two minutes. Place a slice of herb butter on each scallop and cook for a further one minute, making sure the herbs do not burn. Serve immediately.

THE LEMON TREE
268 Woodstock Road, Oxford OX2 7NW
Tel: 01865 311936

Braised shoulder of Cornish lamb with Caponata, herbed potatoes, lamb reduction

INGREDIENTS

1 boned and rolled lamb shoulder noisette	1 bulb garlic, crushed	1tbsp tomato purée
1 onion, chopped	1 bay leaf	500ml red wine
1 carrot, chopped	Sprig rosemary	300ml dark chicken stock
3 sticks celery, chopped	$1/_2$ bunch mint	200ml veal stock
	10 peppercorns	

METHOD

In a heavy pan or roasting dish cook the vegetables in a little olive oil or fat, until lightly browned, over a medium heat.

Add the lamb and colour the skin, then add the tomato purée, wine, stock and herbs, scraping any caramelised bits from the bottom of the dish with a wooden spoon.

Place uncovered in a preheated oven at 150°C and cook for three and a half to four hours until the lamb is tender.

Take out the lamb and cool. Pass the cooling liquid through a sieve into a clean saucepan and reduce by two thirds or until desired sauce consistency has been achieved.

INGREDIENTS

Caponata

1 large Spanish onion, diced	225g stoned green olives, chopped	**Herbed potatoes**
4 cloves garlic, finely chopped	5 ripe tomatoes, chopped	16 new potatoes
4 celery stalks, diced	200ml red wine vinegar	Handful chopped herbs – parsley, chervil, chives, mint, basil
1kg aubergine, diced	2tbsp capers	Good quality olive oil
2 courgettes, diced	2tbsp caster sugar	Salt and pepper
1 large red pepper, diced	Olive oil	
1 large yellow pepper, diced	Salt and pepper	
	Handful chopped coriander and flat parsley	

METHOD

Caponata is a vegetable stew from Sicily, made traditionally from just aubergine and courgettes. We have added peppers, not just for complementing flavours but also the fantastic colours. It can be eaten hot or cold, and will keep for at least a week in the fridge, where flavours will improve.

Heat about four tbsp olive oil in a large frying pan and cook the onions until soft and translucent.

Add the garlic and tomatoes raise the heat and cook until you have a thick paste.

Add the capers, celery, olives, vinegar and sugar and simmer over a low heat for 15-20 minutes. Transfer into a bowl. Heat another four tbsp oil over a medium heat and fry the aubergines until soft and golden brown and stir into the onion mix.

Repeat the process with the peppers and courgettes, season to taste and mix in the herbs.

Herbed potatoes

Boil the potatoes in salted water until soft, drain and gently crush in a bowl with back of a spoon. Mix in the herbs and 3-4 tbsp olive oil. Season to taste.

To serve

Cut the lamb into four pieces and place in a pan with a little oil and butter.

Roast in a hot oven for 10-15 minutes, turning occasionally until the outside is golden brown and crispy. Rest for five minutes. Whilst the meat is resting reheat the Caponata, potatoes and sauce in separate pans. Arrange the potato and Caponata into two piles on a warm plate and sit the lamb on top. Spoon the sauce around.

THE LEMON TREE
268 Woodstock Road, Oxford OX2 7NW
Tel: 01865 311936

Chocolate pudding with cherries marinated in kirsch, white chocolate ice cream

You need an ice cream maker for this recipe.

Chocolate pudding

125g butter plus a little more to grease the ramekins

2tbsp flour (plus a little more to line the ramekins)

125g 70 per cent dark chocolate

3 eggs

1 egg yolk

5tbsp caster sugar

To serve

12 cherries marinated in kirsch

4 scoops white chocolate ice cream

Marinated cherries

1kg cherries, stoned

250g caster sugar

250ml water

500ml kirsch

White chocolate ice cream

500ml milk

500ml double cream

100g caster sugar

12 egg yolks

1 vanilla pod

200g good quality white chocolate

White chocolate ice cream

Halve the vanilla pod and place in a pan with the milk and cream.

Bring to just below the boil. Mix the egg yolks and sugar together in a bowl.

Slowly pour in the hot liquid, stirring constantly. Pour back into the pan and cook on a very low heat, stirring all the time with a wooden spoon or plastic spatula until it starts to thicken. Do not allow to boil. Pour through a sieve in to a bowl and leave to cool.

Place a small pan of water on to boil and put a metal or glass bowl on the top making sure it is not touching the water. Melt the white chocolate in the bowl and add to the ice cream mix. Place the mix into an ice cream maker and follow the manufacturer's instructions for churning. Alternatively, buy a top quality white chocolate ice cream!

Marinated cherries

Dissolve the sugar and water and bring to the boil. Add the cherries and the kirsch, simmer for 2-3 minutes. Seal in airtight glass jars until needed. They keep for several weeks in the fridge.

Chocolate pudding

To make the pudding preheat the oven to 220°C. Liberally butter and flour the ramekins. Melt the chocolate over simmering water in a metal or glass bowl. Whisk the eggs and sugar together to a thick but light consistency. Pour in the chocolate and sieve in the flour. Fold together and spoon or pipe into the dishes. Cook for 10-12 mins. Serve immediately with the ice cream and cherries. The puddings can be served in the dishes or turned out.

THE LEMON TREE
268 Woodstock Road, Oxford OX2 7NW
Tel: 01865 311936

MEDIO

MEDIO

The recently refurbished Medio restaurant is a stylish and modern dining experience with a superbly crafted brasserie menu, offering classic ingredients with a contemporary twist and a refreshing wine selection.

The Medio menu is a reflection of the cosmopolitan mix in our brigade of young chefs who are only too happy to show off their creativity and international influences in fresh combinations and very different styles.

The Medio restaurant is located in The Oxford Hotel, just north of Oxford.

The hotel has recently undergone an extensive £12 million refurbishment and boasts fantastic contemporary design in all areas – making it well worth the visit. The doors are open to all customers anytime – families included! If you prefer a more informal and leisurely lunch we also offer a variety of speciality coffees, cakes and light lunches in the Cappuccino Bar.

Keeping in mind the hospitality ethic of a full service four star hotel, we strive to provide all of our guests with a truly exceptional experience, which is achieved by creating a beautiful environment, fantastic food, good wine and most importantly personal service from a friendly and happy team.

We look forward to sharing the Medio experience with you!

The Medio team

Rocket salad topped with goat's cheese and finished with balsamic dressing

INGREDIENTS

4tbsp balsamic vinegar

10g sugar

1 large bunch of fresh rocket salad

3 fresh figs

4tsp honey

100g goat's cheese

$1^1/_2$tsp mustard

6tbsp olive oil

Salt and pepper seasoning

A selection of fresh peppers thinly cut into strips

METHOD

Heat the balsamic vinegar and the sugar in a pan to make a thick reduction.

Pick fresh leaves of rocket salad and place in chilled water.

Quarter the figs and pour the honey over each piece. Glaze under a medium grill until a golden colour is achieved.

Slice and place the goat's cheese on a non stick baking tray and bake in a pre-heated oven on 180°C for one minute. This is to soften and colour the cheese.

Whisk the olive oil into the mustard to make a dressing. Add salt and pepper to taste.

Place the rocket in the centre of the plate and decorate the figs around the salad. Place the goat's cheese on top of the salad and dress with the mustard dressing. Finish with the balsamic reduction and place the shredded peppers on top.

MEDIO
The Oxford Hotel, Godstow Road, Oxford OX2 8AL
Tel: 01865 489937
www.paramount-hotels.co.uk

Roast English salmon and king prawn hollandaise

INGREDIENTS

4 x 150g un-skinned salmon fillets

12 king prawn tails shelled

12 broccoli florets

4 turned carrots

4 asparagus spears

1 clove garlic

2tbsp lemon juice

Dill leaves for decoration

Salt and pepper

Olive oil

Spring onion mashed potatoes

4 medium jacket potatoes

2tbsp double cream

1tbsp butter

3tsp chopped spring onion

Red wine sauce

1oz butter

1tsp finely chopped thyme

170ml red wine

100ml red wine vinegar

Salt and freshly milled pepper

Hollandaise sauce

3 large egg yolks

1tbsp lemon juice

110g butter

1tbsp white wine vinegar

Salt and freshly milled pepper

METHOD

Boil potatoes until soft and then peel away the skin.

Rub the salmon fillets with lemon juice and season with salt and pepper. Make an X mark on the skin side of the fillet and bake in a pre-heated oven at 150°C leave this for 10-15 minutes.

Melt butter for red wine sauce in saucepan and add thyme. Add red wine and red wine vinegar, season and gently bring to boil. Leave simmering for 10 minutes to reduce.

Place egg yolks for hollandaise sauce in small bowl, season and mix thoroughly. Heat the lemon juice and white wine vinegar in a small saucepan, until it starts to bubble. Pour liquid slowly onto egg yolks in slow stream.

Using the same saucepan, melt butter over gentle heat. Once foaming pour butter slowly into mix and blend to yield smooth buttery sauce.

Place potatoes in a large pot and add the butter and spring onions. Use a masher to mash the potatoes until smooth. Fold in the cream.

Blanch broccoli, asparagus and carrots.

Pour a little olive oil in a hot frying pan and add the garlic. Fry the prawn tails for two minutes on each side until bright pink.

Spoon the hollandaise sauce onto the serving plate and place the salmon and a large spoon of mashed potatoes on the plate. Arrange the vegetables around this, add the prawns for decoration and finish with the red wine sauce and dill leaves.

MEDIO

The Oxford Hotel, Godstow Road, Oxford OX2 8AL

Tel: 01865 489937

www.paramount-hotels.co.uk

Pear Martini

100g rice	Ground cinnamon
1.5 litre milk	2 cinnamon sticks
Peel of 1 large lemon	6 pears
350g sugar	1 litre water
1tsp vanilla essence	8oz dark chocolate

Heat the milk with half of the lemon peel and one cinnamon stick. Bring to the boil and add the rice, then turn down the heat to a gentle simmer and stir constantly.

Once the rice is cooked, add 250g of sugar and stir. The rice normally takes 20-30 minutes to cook. If it reduces too quickly you may add extra milk. Once cooked set aside.

Break the chocolate into a heat-proof bowl/double boiler. Melt the chocolate very slowly over a pan of gently simmering water. Stir well until smooth.

Peel the pears and take out the seeds, place into a pan with the water, 100g of sugar and the vanilla essence.

Once the pears are soft take them out of the water, drip dry and fill the hollows with melted chocolate.

Place the pears in the fridge for an hour.

Place a single pear in the middle of a Martini glass. Spoon some of the rice pudding neatly into the glass surrounding the pear.

Sprinkle with cinnamon and decorate with a piece of cinnamon stick and lemon peel.

MEDIO

The Oxford Hotel, Godstow Road, Oxford OX2 8AL
Tel: 01865 489937
www.paramount-hotels.co.uk

THE MOLE AND CHICKEN

Manageress Kelly Cherry with Shane Ellis

THE MOLE AND CHICKEN

The Mole and Chicken is a charming country restaurant set in a quiet Buckinghamshire hamlet, overlooking magnificent views of the Thames Valley. It was a nineteenth century former village store built to supply the workers' estate and was licensed to sell ale and cider from 1918.

The tastefully decorated open-plan interior with its oak and pine tables, rag washed terracotta walls, log fires, candlelight and flagged floors offer a warm welcome. The atmosphere is relaxed and chatty and served by friendly staff with generous helpings of imaginative food from our traditional English menu.

As winners of Bucks Dining Pub of the Year 2003 we are a popular local gastro pub and believe that your meal should be a sensory experience, a combination of aromas, colours and taste. We always source new products for the changing menus, chosen for their seasonal freshness which are complemented by our extensive wine and malt whisky lists.

Next door, Leanne runs the B&B with five delightful and comfortably furnished rooms, and she and Kelly, the manageress, are the driving force behind the great service and ambience provided at The Mole.

Shane Ellis
The Mole and Chicken

Wok-cooked sweet chilli mussels

2kg live mussels, debearded

Olive oil

1 clove of chopped garlic

2 fresh chillies, sliced, red or green

Sweet chilli dipping sauce

1 bunch fresh chopped coriander

5 spring onions, finely sliced

2 limes, juiced

100ml dry white wine

200ml double cream

This dish takes literally minutes to cook and adds an interesting twist to a popular dish. Simply serve with crusty bread.

Place your mussels and a drizzle of olive oil into a large hot wok. Add the garlic, spring onions, wine and chillis and keep turning the mussels until they are all opened, discarding any that remain closed. Squeeze in the limes and add the cream and sweet chilli sauce. Garnish with coriander and serve immediately with crusty bread.

THE MOLE AND CHICKEN
Easington Terrace, Long Crendon, Aylesbury HP18 9EY
Tel: 01844 208387
www.moleandchicken.co.uk

Gressingham duck with a honey and orange sauce

INGREDIENTS

2 Gressingham ducks, 1.8kg each, to serve four

Mache to garnish

200ml warm vegetable stock

Juice and rind of four oranges

2tbsp honey

1tbsp plain flour

METHOD

If possible try to use fresh duck. The weight of a duck is important because to get a crispy skin and moist meat finish it needs to be cooked long and slow, and the weight of the bird will be greatly reduced by the end of the cooking time. You may need a bigger bird than you think. We recommend you cook it for about 30 minutes per half kilo so that most of the fat will be rendered down.

Pre-heat the oven to 200°C. Place the duck on a tray in the roasting tin. Pat it dry with paper towel and make sure the giblets are removed. Don't add any oil or fat to the duck; it has enough of its own. After 20 minutes turn your oven down to 180°C and leave the duck for about three hours. When the cooking time is up remove the duck from the pan, pouring the excess fat into a bowl, it is lovely for roasting potatoes on Sunday.

Leave the bird to relax for five minutes and then using kitchen scissors divide it into portions and serve with delicious honey and orange sauce. Garnish with sliced orange and a bunch of mache.

Sauce

Spoon out some of the excess fat from the roasting tin and stir in the flour to make a paste. Over a low heat add the warm vegetable stock gradually and stir continuously to make a smooth sauce. Cook for a minute and then add the honey and orange for a lovely bittersweet sauce to complement the full flavour of the duck.

THE MOLE AND CHICKEN
Easington Terrace, Long Crendon, Aylesbury HP18 9EY
Tel: 01844 208387
www.moleandchicken.co.uk

Honey and walnut cheesecake

INGREDIENTS

150ml double cream

150g mascapone cheese

150g cream cheese

2tbsp honey

200g crushed walnuts

Rind and juice of 1 lemon

200g digestive biscuits

100g butter

Fresh berries of choice

Ice cream

METHOD

This is a simple and delicious recipe and can be easily adapted to suit any taste.

To make the base, crush the biscuits to a fine crumb. Melt the butter and mix together with the crumbs. Pack evenly into three-inch pastry rounds and refrigerate until firm.

Whip the cream until it peaks and fold in the mascarpone and cream cheese. Add the honey and lemon to taste depending on how sweet your tooth. Spoon the mixture into the pastry rounds being careful to leave no air pockets. Wrap a warm cloth around the pastry round and gently remove it leaving your single serve cheesecake on the plate. Sprinkle the crushed walnut on top and garnish with some fresh berries and perhaps a scoop of ice cream.

THE MOLE AND CHICKEN
Easington Terrace, Long Crendon, Aylesbury HP18 9EY
Tel: 01844 208387
www.moleandchicken.co.uk

OLD PARSONAGE

Head chef Daniel Norland

OLD PARSONAGE

A haven of tranquillity, the Old Parsonage is a thoroughly grown-up establishment conveniently located a short walk from the city centre and less than an hour from London – a country retreat despite its urban location. A real fire burns in the lobby all year round, and 'traditional-meets-modern' best describes the decor in the 30-room hotel situated over two floors around a herb-planted roof garden.

The Parsonage Bar and Restaurant has the intimate appeal of a private members club. It is open from breakfast to 11pm daily serving modern British classic dishes, with emphasis on fresh local ingredients. Whether it's the simplicity of a good steak and chips, stunning seafood imported from Jersey or a lobster salad in summer, the Parsonage delivers quality food and service with great style.

From June to the end of September there is a nightly barbeque on the front terrace accompanied by live jazz on Fridays. Whenever possible, chefs use high quality, free-range, organic produce sourced from individual fishermen, farmers and producers. Enjoy breakfast, lunch, the Old Parsonage famous afternoon tea, dinner or just a drink and a snack at the Old Parsonage.

Marie Jackson
General manager, the Old Parsonage

Twice baked spinach and parmesan soufflé

INGREDIENTS

125g spinach (finely sliced)	45g grated Parmesan
400ml milk	Pinch nutmeg
75g unsalted butter	Salt and pepper to taste
55g plain flour	Double cream
4 large eggs separated	
45g grated Cheddar	Leaf salad to serve

METHOD

Butter eight small ramekins and set to one side. Melt butter in a pan and mix in flour to make a roux. Cook for two minutes stirring continuously, then remove from heat and in a separate pan heat milk until almost boiling and add spinach. Bring to the boil then add slowly to the roux stirring all the time. While still hot add the Cheddar, Parmesan, salt, pepper and nutmeg. Finally add the egg yolks and mix until smooth. Leave to cool.

Whisk the egg whites to stiff peaks and fold carefully into the rest of the ingredients.

Spoon into the ramekins and bake in a bain marie at 200°C for 15 to 20 minutes or until spongy to touch. Remove from oven and leave to cool.

Turn out soufflés into an ovenproof dish, pour a small amount of double cream over each soufflé. Sprinkle with grated Parmesan and bake in a hot oven for 10 to 15 minutes or until browned on top. Serve with a dressed leaf salad.

OLD PARSONAGE
1 Banbury Road, Oxford OX2 6NN
Tel: 01865 310210
www.oldparsonage-hotel.co.uk

Rump of lamb with roast peppers, aubergine crisps and rosemary jus

INGREDIENTS

8 (250g) lamb rump steaks

3 red and 3 yellow peppers

3 red onions

1 aubergine

24 new potatoes

Garlic for marinade

4 cloves of garlic

Bunch of thyme

6tbsp extra virgin olive oil

Bunch of rosemary

$1/_2$ pint lamb stock

Salt and black pepper

Caster sugar

For lamb stock

750g lamb rib or neck bones

2tbsp olive oil

2 carrots

1 stick of celery

$1/_2$ head of garlic

1tbsp tomato purée

1 bay leaf

4 sprigs rosemary

3 pints of water

8oz red wine

METHOD

Marinate lamb in olive oil, garlic and rosemary overnight.

For lamb stock you can buy ready-made decent lamb stock or make your own as follows: Roast off lamb bones in olive oil for 50 mins at 200°C. Meanwhile heat oil in large saucepan and add coarsely chopped vegetables and sweat on a medium heat for 15 minutes. Add the red wine and reduce liquid by half. Add tomato puree bay leaf, rosemary, roasted lamb bones and water. Bring to boil and gently simmer for three hours. Allow liquid to reduce by two thirds. Skim fat off the stock then strain through a fine chinoise or muslin. Leave to cool.

For the aubergine crisp thinly slice the aubergine, using a mandolin if you have one.

Lay out slices on a wire rack and sprinkle lightly with equal quantities of salt and caster sugar on both sides. Set aside for 15 minutes to allow bitter water to be drawn out.

De-seed peppers and slice length ways into quarters and roughly slice the red onion. Crush garlic and chop thyme.

Turn all the potatoes until equal size and par boil for 10 minutes.

Add peppers, onion, garlic and thyme and seasoning to hot olive oil in an ovenproof dish and roast in a pre-heated oven at 200°C for 25 minutes.

Sear lamb in a hot pan on the hob until brown and place steaks and turned potatoes in a large roasting dish. Cook in oven at 200°C for 20 minutes for medium cooked.

Wipe the aubergine slices with kitchen paper and gently fry in olive oil until crisp.

Finally remove lamb and potatoes from oven and set lamb aside to rest (five minutes) deglaze roasting dish with half pint of lamb stock and reduce by half.

To present the dish, slice lamb steaks through and arrange on top of peppers and aubergine with three potatoes per person, spoon reduced stock over the dish and a rosemary sprig for a garnish.

OLD PARSONAGE
1 Banbury Road, Oxford OX2 6NN
Tel: 01865 310210
www.oldparsonage-hotel.co.uk

Banana and rum baked Alaska

Ice cream

3 ripe bananas

260g dark brown sugar

120ml milk

120ml double cream

2 pints double cream lightly whipped

4 egg yolks

4tbsp dark rum

Alaska sponge base

95g dark brown sugar

3 large eggs

95g plain flour (sifted)

Meringue

4 egg whites

225g caster sugar

Pinch of salt

Teaspoon lemon juice

Ice cream

Purée bananas with 130g dark brown sugar until smooth. Add rum and set aside. Whisk egg yolks and 130g of dark brown sugar. Slowly add milk and cream and whisk until thick. Add to puréed bananas and fold mixture into two pints of lightly whipped cream. Churn ingredients in ice-cream maker or freeze in container and whisk after one hour.

Sponge base

Whisk eggs and sugar until very light and fluffy. Slowly fold in sifted flour. Spread mixture evenly over a baking tray lined with baking parchment until it is two cm thick. Bake in a pre-heated oven at 200°C for 15 minutes until firm. Once cooked and slightly cooled cut out bases with an 8cm circular cutter.

Meringue

Whisk egg white and lemon juice until peaks are stiff. Add salt and slowly incorporate sugar whilst still whisking.

To build the Alaska place a large scoop of ice cream on each base and return to the freezer for 15 minutes. Fill piping bag with meringue and pipe mixture onto ice cream until it is completely covered (see picture of spiked peaks). Keep in freezer until ready to bake.

To serve place Alaska on a baking tray lined with baking parchment and dust with icing sugar. Bake in a pre-heated oven at maximum temperature for two-three minutes or until meringue starts to brown. Serve immediately.

OLD PARSONAGE

1 Banbury Road, Oxford OX2 6NN

Tel: 01865 310210

www.oldparsonage-hotel.co.uk

THE OLIVE

THE OLIVE

Authenticity, originality and freshness are the three key ingredients for food at The Olive. Researching local food traditions and ingredients is a central aspect of our work and we aim to collaborate with local producers in developing food that combine flavour and innovation. The restaurant is situated in the heart of the picturesque North Oxfordshire village of Deddington in a Grade II listed building noted for its unusual structure.

Our young head chef Stuart James provides exciting and ambitious dishes on a modern British theme with a French influence. Freshness and simplicity are central to his cooking style.

The fine eating experience is enhanced by relaxing atmosphere and traditional countryside hospitality. We offer fixed price menus for lunch and dinner and seasonal specials.

If you love Oxfordshire, you will love The Olive.

Jean-Pierre Garnier
www.theoliverestaurant.co.uk

Pork and sage terrine with cherry mustard

INGREDIENTS

Forcemeat

1kg minced British pork belly (lean/fat ratio: 50/50)

200g chicken liver

150g chopped onion

30ml cooking brandy

50g pistachio nuts

20g chopped fresh English garden sage

2 eggs

30g plain flour

Salt, pepper, mace, ginger, all spice

Pinch of saltpeter (potassium nitrate)

Butter

Sage stuffing

150g fresh English garden sage

150g New Zealand spinach (tetragonia) or young nettle leaves

1 whole egg

1 egg white

Cherry mustard (for 1kg, can be stored)

430g natural colour glacé cherries

200g yellow mustard seeds

100g black mustard seeds

30g mustard powder

50g coriander seeds

20g white pepper corns

120ml raspberry vinegar

50ml dry sherry

METHOD

This is a wonderful combination of traditional English flavour and French charcuterie technique. As an alternative to the sage mixture, the terrine may be lined with blanched sage leaves and incorporate a layer of sage leaves in the centre.

For the sage mixture, take the stalks off the sage and spinach leaves. Blanch very quickly. Chop and press in a cloth to extract excess water. Incorporate the eggs in the mixture.

Sweat the chopped onion in hot butter until golden. Flash-fry the chicken liver in hot pan with butter and when cooled down chop. In a mixing bowl blend the pork, brandy, onion, chicken liver and salt. Blend in the beaten eggs. Mix the flour with all other dry ingredients and incorporate in the forcemeat. Cover and leave to cure overnight at around 5°C. Line the dish with clingfilm. Fill with a layer of the forcemeat then a layer of the sage mixture, then a layer of forcemeat. Cover with film. Put the terrine in an oven dish in a bain-marie. Cover the oven dish with foil. Cook for approximately four hours at 95°C to reach a temperature of 68-70°C in the centre. Take out of the oven and leave to set for one hour. Put some weight on the terrine to press. Cool overnight in the fridge. Turn out the following day. The terrine is ready for slicing.

For the cherry mustard, crush the seeds coarsely in a mortar, add the vinegar and the mustard powder. Chop the cherries in a blender. Mix the crushed seeds with the cherries and finish with the sherry. The mustard stores well and improves after a week.

THE OLIVE
Market Place, Deddington, Oxfordshire OX15 OSE
Tel: 01869 338813
www.theoliverestaurant.co.uk

Braised pheasant with caramelised apples and shallots

INGREDIENTS

2 pheasants, well hung

28 shallots

3 apples, peeled and sliced into eighths

12 new potatoes

1 sliced carrot

Parsley stalks

$1/_2$ bottle of strong red wine

30 ml of red wine vinegar

One sprig of thyme and rosemary, bay leaf

Flour

Butter

Salt and crushed black pepper

Demerara sugar

Chopped parsley

METHOD

Oxfordshire is blessed with an abundance of game in season, particularly pheasant. This winter dish, popular with our customers, has what it takes to feature on a restaurant menu: it tastes and looks good.

Skin the pheasant, and bone-out the breast and leg. If you are unsure how to do this, ask your butcher to do it for you.

Trim the meat and remove the bloody parts. Check for shot. Cut the boneless meat into large chunks. In a thick pan, sweat four finely chopped shallots in hot butter. Add the meat and brown. Add the red wine, parsley, carrot slices, vinegar and seasoning. Gently simmer for approximately 45 minutes. Take the meat out, strain the sauce then introduce the meat back with the sauce. Brown the cored apples, which should be previously sliced into eighths, and 24 peeled shallots in hot butter and sugar. Parboil the new potatoes, cool, cut in halves then deep fry. On a large plate, present the pheasant in the centre and alternate six apple slices, six shallots and six potato halves. To finish, sprinkle with chopped parsley.

THE OLIVE
Market Place, Deddington, Oxfordshire OX15 0SE
Tel: 01869 338813
www.theoliverestaurant.co.uk

Salami of dry fruits with Drambuie syrup

Dry fruit salami

400g soft dry figs	
70g stoned dates	
50g candied lemon peel	
50g almond powder	
50g flaked almonds	
500g pistachio nuts	
30ml Drambuie liqueur	
30ml cooking brandy	
Roasted flaked almonds	

Vanilla pod

Sliced ginger

Rice paper

Drambuie syrup

200ml cane syrup	
Lemon and orange peel	
$1/_2$ vanilla pod	
Sliced ginger	
60ml Drambuie	

Needs to be prepared at least 48 hours in advance.

This original dessert has a superb taste and an unusual presentation. Fans of Drambuie liqueur will not be disappointed.

Cut off the hard stalks from the figs. Chop finely in blender. Chop the dates separately in the blender. In a mixing bowl, blend the remaining ingredients, finishing with the liquid. Roll the fig mix onto rice paper as a log. Wrap in cling film. Refrigerate for 48 hours to cool and set. Taking off the wrapping film, slice and garnish with pine nuts and roasted flaked almonds.

For the Drambuie sauce, mix the cane syrup with the ingredients in a pan and simmer gently. Cool down slightly. Add the Drambuie. Flambé to burn the alcohol, strain, then cool down.

THE OLIVE

Market Place, Deddington, Oxfordshire OX15 OSE
Tel: 01869 338813
www.theoliverestaurant.co.uk

QUOD

QUOD

Right in the heart of Oxford, Quod Restaurant & Bar opened in November 1999 as part of the Old Bank Hotel. The impressive Georgian banking hall lends itself to a vibrant restaurant, which serves a popular Italian-inspired menu with the emphasis on quality food, both affordable and accessible. But there's more to the dining experience at Quod than the cuisine.

A fantastic collection of 20th century art showcases some of Britain's foremost up and coming young artists. You can't fail to be impressed by the array of huge paintings hanging on the walls.

Quod is an exciting concept, with a relaxed informal bar serving coffee, tea, cocktails and an extensive selection of wines. The menu features a varied choice of fresh fish, chargrilled meat, pastas, pizzas and risottos. Head chef Chris Kennedy strives to create exciting dishes using traditional Italian ingredients mixed with fresh local produce where possible

The interior styling uses earthy colours and natural materials such as stone, leather, zinc and oak. An expanse of limestone floor is broken up by the zinc-topped bar and the restaurant itself retains original features from the bank, such as the stone archway that once led to the safe.

The summer months offer al fresco dining on the large terrace where you can enjoy a sun drenched lunch or a leisurely sip on your favourite cocktail, where the gentle waterfall adds to the ambience.

There is also the option of private dining in The Red Room, which offers the ideal venue for celebrations, business dinners and conferences.

Children of all ages are welcome in the restaurant and have a menu prepared especially for them.

Quod looks forward to welcoming you soon.

Seafood risotto

160g risotto rice

1tbsp oil

1 litre fish stock

40g prawn tails

12g chopped parsley

pinch saffron

60ml white wine

4tbsp white wine vinegar

1tbsp garlic oil

1tsp chilli oil

60g sliced squid

12 clams

12 mussels

4 king prawns

12 cherry tomatoes, halved

2oz butter

Salt and pepper

Coat the rice in a little oil or butter in a large pan and heat through for a couple of minutes. Add 20ml of the white wine and allow to be absorbed. Keep adding one ladle of stock, allowing absorption each time, until rice is al dente. This should take around 20 minutes. Keep a little stock back.

Take off the heat.

In another pan put the garlic oil, chilli oil, mussels, clams, squid and king prawns. Add 40ml white wine, a little stock, then cover until all the shells are open. Add cherry tomatoes, chopped parsley and half the butter. Remove from heat.

Reheat rice, add saffron, vinegar, prawn tails, salt and pepper. Remove from heat. Add rest of butter and mix with wooden spoon until smooth and creamy.

Put rice in centre of plate. Pour over stock, then place shells, squid and tomatoes on top of the rice.

QUOD
92-94 High Street, Oxford OX1 4BN
Tel: 01865 202505

Duck confit

INGREDIENTS

1.4kg duck leg confit

30g lard

2tbsp vegetable oil

1tbsp fresh thyme

1tbsp fresh rosemary

2 cloves chopped garlic

60g halved cherry tomatoes

40g sliced prune lardons

40g pancetta lardons

3 spring onions, sliced

20g chopped parsley

20g unsalted butter

80ml white wine

80ml demiglace

Salt and pepper

**240g mashed celeriac (prepare
two or three days in advance)**

1tbsp milk

30g butter

1tbsp chopped sage

METHOD

Place the duck in a deep baking tray with lard, vegetable oil, thyme, rosemary and chopped garlic. Cover and cook at 260°C for two to three hours, until duck is nearly coming off the bone.

Leave to cool down in oil and lard. Best left for two to three days.

Celeriac mash

Peel and dice celeriac. Cover with milk, butter, salt and pepper. Cook until soft, then mash and add chopped sage.

When ready to serve duck, cook at 350°C for 10-15 minutes. After three minutes, pour off excess oil. Keep pouring off oil at intervals until skin is crispy.

Serve on top of celeriac mash.

Heat pan with a little oil, add pancetta and prunes and sauté until crispy. Add white wine and take off heat. Add demiglace, cherry tomatoes and spring onions and butter. Stir in until thick sauce, add parsley and serve over the duck.

QUOD
92-94 High Street, Oxford OX1 4BN
Tel: 01865 202505

Tiramisu

INGREDIENTS

15 egg whites

$^1/_2$ pint double cream

500g mascarpone cheese

100g icing sugar

150ml Marsala wine

330g Savoyarde biscuits

1 litre diluted espresso coffee

20g bitter cocoa powder

Chocolate sauce (for decoration)

METHOD

Whisk egg whites until stiff peaks are formed. Put aside.

Whisk double cream until at ribbing stage. Then add sugar, Marsala and whisk slowly until mixed.

Fold in mascarpone and egg whites and two shots of espresso coffee.

Start soaking Savoyarde biscuits in cold black coffee, then lay in a tray.

Spoon over half the cream mix, then another layer of Savoyarde on top. Smooth out the rest of the cream mix and dust with cocoa powder.

Chill.

Serve on a plate drizzled with chocolate.

QUOD
92-94 High Street, Oxford OX1 4BN
Tel: 01865 202505

SIP RESTAURANT & BAR

*Jay and Brinley
Green, with
head chef
Jonathan Wilmot*

SIP RESTAURANT & BAR

SIP... what a great name for a bar.

Brothers Jay and Brinley Green teamed up to open a modern bar and restaurant in Oxford's popular Jericho district. Working closely together in this brand new venture, they have brought in the expertise of design group Din Associates to create a space that is minimal and an atmosphere that is intimate.

The stunning white modern frontage is a welcoming oasis on Walton Street.

A sleek interior boasts a cool contemporary charcoal limestone floor and ebony fittings.

A lilac halo of soft light eminates from the bar area, creating a chic and subtle effect.

The bar menu is concise and simple, complementing perfectly an exciting and extensive drinks list.

Beyond the bar is a contemporary restaurant with 50 covers – ten of these on the terrace. Here you will find a wonderfully eclectic menu borrowed from around the world.

Open for lunch through to dinner everyday, SIP is waiting to welcome you.

Brinley and Jay Green, SIP

Sweet pepper, pine nut and goat's cheese won-tons

INGREDIENTS

50ml olive oil

3 small peppers, (1 red, 1 yellow and 1 green)

70g pine nuts

125g goat's cheese

10g picked thyme

1 packet won-ton papers

Salt and pepper

10ml balsamic vinegar

METHOD

The mixture of oriental won-ton papers with a very European filling make this light starter a good way to begin cooking with an unfamiliar ingredient.

Peel the peppers using a vegetable peeler. Try to remove as much of the bitter skin as possible but due to the shape you will be unable to remove it all. Chop into 1cm squares and place in a baking tray with the olive oil, thyme and seasoning. Place in the middle of an oven pre-heated to 160°C. They should take about 40 minutes to become soft, but not really take on any colour.

Meanwhile brown your pine nuts in a separate pan to the peppers in the oven for 10 minutes. Slice or crumble your goat's cheese into small pieces.

Once you have taken your peppers out of the oven remove them from most of the oil which they have been cooked in, add the vinegar, cheese and nuts. The filling is now complete.

All that remains is to place a small amount of mixture into the centre of each won-ton skin, moisten the edges and then gathering the four corners twisting it into a parcel. Deep-fry these until golden in oil at 170°C.

Serve immediately with a sweet chilli dipping sauce and crisp salad.

SIP RESTAURANT & BAR
102 Walton Street, Jericho, Oxford OX2 6EB
Tel: 01865 311322
www.barsip.com

Poached fillet of beef salad
with stir-fried young vegetables

INGREDIENTS

For the marinade

30ml soy sauce (in the kitchen we always use Kikkoman)

1 star anise

5g Chinese five spice

300ml red wine

1 stalk of lemongrass

25g root ginger

1 chilli

For the salad

4 x 100g fillet of beef

250g sugar snap peas

250g baby sweet corn

12 asparagus spears

300-400g mixed salad (we use roquette, baby spinach and radicchio)

Salt

For the dressing

15ml soy sauce

15ml olive oil

15ml lime juice

15ml sesame oil

METHOD

This is a fantastic way to cook beef really well for people who are not confident of cooking steak, yet it tastes absolutely amazing.

Combine all the ingredients for the marinade. Bash the lemongrass to release its flavours, discarding the outer husk and chopping into 2cm pieces, and roughly slice the chilli, removing the seeds. Now place the beef in the marinade for at least four hours, but preferably overnight. At this point you can also make your dressing by combining all the ingredients and leaving in the fridge.

When your beef has marinated sufficiently remove it from the liquid and place to one side. Transfer the liquid to a pan over a moderate heat and bring to a simmer. Meanwhile in a separate pan bring some salted water to a rapid boil. Check that the asparagus has been trimmed of any of the excessively woody stalk and place in the water for three mins. Remove and refresh under cold running water.

Now bring a large sauté pan, or wok, up to a very high temperature. By this time your poaching liquor for the beef should have reached temperature and be reducing slightly. Place all of the marinated beef into it for five minutes. Remove and allow to rest on a chopping board. Into your now very hot sauté pan place all of your vegetables with a little olive oil and stir-fry until slightly softened, around four minutes.

Serve by placing the dressed salad inside a ring of the vegetables in the centre of a large plate. Place the beef, sliced in two, on top of the salad and drizzle with any remaining dressing.

SIP RESTAURANT & BAR
102 Walton Street, Jericho, Oxford OX2 6EB
Tel: 01865 311322
www.barsip.com

Melting chocolate fondants

INGREDIENTS

4 eggs

2 egg yolks

$^1/_2$tsp baking powder

125g butter (preferably unsalted)

125g cocoa solids (70%) dark chocolate

25g cocoa powder

75g plain flour

250g golden caster sugar

150ml double cream to serve

METHOD

These fantastically rich puddings are ideal for entertaining as they can be made ahead. Also because they rise in the oven they have a slightly 'soufflé' effect which is bound to impress your guests.

Melt chocolate and butter together in a glass bowl, over a pan of barely simmering water.

Meanwhile combine eggs, egg yolks and sugar together and beat with a balloon whisk until beginning to form ribbons, around two minutes of vigorous work. Now gently fold in the chocolate mixture. Finally, sieve in your remaining dry ingredients and using the balloon whisk mix until smooth and glossy.

Now divide the mixture between four coffee cups – you should only fill them to 2cm from the top, as your mixture will rise in the oven. You can now chill your desserts, for up to 24 hours, before baking them for around 14 minutes at 180°C. The ideal fondant will have an almost liquid centre that should still be obvious when you serve it to your guests with cold double cream.

SIP RESTAURANT & BAR
102 Walton Street, Jericho, Oxford OX2 6EB
Tel: 01865 311322
www.barsip.com

SIXTY SIX A

Hotel manager Paul Peros with head chef Garin Chapman

SIXTY SIX A

Under the watchful and experienced eye of Savoy-trained head chef Garin Chapman the Cotswold Lodge Hotel has been working hard to bring its unique blend of style, elegance and classic cuisine to a wider audience.

"Our main aim in the creation of the new menu at Sixty Six A was to offer quality and variety of menu that was accessible to all."

Despite the creation of value meals that offer a two-course working lunch and drink for under £10 the philosophy remains the same.

"We make everything ourselves from the freshest local ingredients. Stocks for sauces, bread rolls for the tables, even the ice creams and after-dinner chocolates are made here."

Diners can choose from the relaxing bar with open fireplace in winter and the newly created walled patio garden for perfect summer al fresco meals. Those wishing to sample the elegance of Sixty Six A's main dining room will be treated to a relaxed and unhurried meal that offers some of the very best in modern European cooking and a selection of wines to compliment. The restaurant has a vibrant atmosphere that belies the sedate surroundings.

With ample free parking and its proximity to the centre of Oxford we think we may have unearthed a little gem at Sixty Six A.

Red snapper and smoked salmon rillettes served with aubergine crisps

INGREDIENTS

500g red snapper fillet, skin on

350g smoked salmon, unsliced and cut into chunks

600ml fish stock

3 bay leaves

350g unsalted butter softened to room temp

1 aubergine

1tbsp crushed green peppercorns

Sea salt

METHOD

Put red snapper fillet, skin side down, in a suitably sized pan and cover with fish stock. Add the bay leaves, heat until simmering and cook for a further five minutes. Remove from heat and allow fish to cool in the stock. Once cooled, remove fish from stock and peel off the skin.

Melt 50g butter in a saucepan and fry smoked salmon until opaque (cooked through and no longer translucent). Allow to cool completely.

With a fork, bind together the red snapper, smoked salmon, peppercorn and softened butter. Season to taste with the sea salt.

Divide into six small dishes and refrigerate until set.

For the crisps, thinly slice the aubergine and deep fry in olive oil until golden brown, place on kitchen paper until cool and crisp. Season with salt.

Take the rillettes out of the fridge 30 minutes before serving, placing the crisps on top.

SIXTY SIX A

The Cotswold Lodge Hotel, 66A Banbury Road, Oxford OX2 6JP
Tel: 01865 512121
www.cotswoldlodgehotel.co.uk

Roast rack of lamb with an apricot, honey and ginger stuffing, served on a red wine sauce

2 large trimmed racks of lamb (ask your butcher to do this)

Stuffing

1 shallot, finely chopped

1cm cube ginger, cut into fine strips

50g dried apricots, roughly chopped

50g butter

25g breadcrumbs

1tsp rosemary, dried or fresh

25g honey

Salt and pepper

Sauce

1 shallot, finely chopped

200ml red wine

200ml beef stock

Salt and pepper

Stuffing

Melt butter in a small saucepan and add the shallot, ginger and rosemary. Cook until soft. Add the apricots and honey, cook for a further two minutes. Add the breadcrumbs and cook until golden brown. Season to taste with salt and pepper and leave to one side.

Lamb

Cut each rack in half and using the handle of a wooden spoon, make a hole through the eye of the meat. Fill the hole with the stuffing and lightly season the meat on both sides.

In a hot roasting tin cook the racks in a pre-heated oven at 180°C for eight minutes, turning halfway through. Once the meat is cooked to your liking, remove from tin and leave to rest.

Sauce

Using excess fat from the roasting tin, heat on the hob adding the shallot and cook until soft.

Add the red wine and reduce by half. Add the beef stock and reduce by half again then season to taste.

Cut the lamb into cutlets and drizzle with the sauce to serve.

SIXTY SIX A

The Cotswold Lodge Hotel, 66A Banbury Road, Oxford OX2 6JP
Tel: 01865 512121
www.cotswoldlodgehotel.co.uk

Sticky toffee pudding with pecan nut sauce

INGREDIENTS

Sponge

75g butter

75g sugar

2 eggs

100g flour

180ml boiling water

$1/_2$tsp vanilla essence

2tsp instant coffee granules

$3/_4$tsp bicarbonate of soda

150g chopped dried dates

Sauce

100g butter

150g Demerara sugar

6tbsp double cream

50g pecan nuts

METHOD

Sponge

Beat the butter and sugar together in a large bowl for two to three minutes until light and fluffy. Add the eggs slowly whilst continually beating. Once all the eggs have been added, fold in all of the flour.

In a separate bowl add the other sponge ingredients and allow to stand for five minutes.

Mix both sets of ingredients together and divide into six lightly greased moulds, filling to about two thirds full. Cover these with lightly greased aluminium foil, place on a tray and bake in a pre-heated oven at 180ºC for 25 minutes.

Sauce

Put all ingredients into a saucepan and slowly bring to the boil. Once the sugar has dissolved, take off the heat and allow to cool for a couple of minutes. Tip out pudding from mould and drizzle with sauce to serve.

SIXTY SIX A

The Cotswold Lodge Hotel, 66A Banbury Road, Oxford OX2 6JP
Tel: 01865 512121
www.cotswoldlodgehotel.co.uk

THE WHITE HART HOTEL

*Eddie Frost,
head chef*

THE WHITE HART HOTEL

A 16th Century coaching inn, The White Hart has an unmistakable character and offers the best of English
hospitality in the ancient village of Dorchester on Thames, just eight miles from the city of Oxford.

The historic setting combines well with the modern British menu created by chef Eddie Frost and his team.
The highest quality fresh produce is used to create innovative and exciting dishes, and there are always fresh
fish and vegetarian options on offer, all supported by good quality and value wines from around the world. The
White Hart is a proud recipient of two AA Rosette awards which reflects the innovative quality of the food.

The high beamed ceiling, separate smoking area, and log fires ensure your comfort, and candle-lit tables
support the warm and intimate ambience. Private dinner parties are welcome in the separate dining room with
its own cheerful log fire and assured high quality personal service.

The White Hart is also fast developing a reputation for combining great dining with live music events
appealing to a wide selection of food and music lovers such as live opera featuring stars of the Welsh National
Opera, jazz from first rate London artistes, and lively Irish music evenings.

Crab rosti cakes

INGREDIENTS

50g picked white crab meat

25g brown crab meat

$1/_2$ finely diced red chilli

1 small piece grated stem ginger

1 egg

$1/_4$ tsp curry powder

$1/_2$ juice of a lime

2dsp chopped fresh coriander

1 good size Maris Piper potato

$1/_2$ clove crushed garlic

Salt and pepper

Dressing

Granny Smith

Basil oil

Pancetta

METHOD

These delicious little morsels form part of a more complex study of crabmeat starter which you can sample at the White Hart. We think you'll enjoy making these, the simplest part of our grand design.

Combine all ingredients together and adjust seasoning. Form into ping pong ball shape, then pat out into a round cake shape about 4cm by $1/_2$cm.

Heat a non-stick frying pan with a little olive oil, gently fry for two minutes each side.

Remove onto a greased tray and finish in the oven 200°C for three-five minutes.

Allow to cool. When ready to serve, reheat at 140°C and plate up with a little dressing and oven-dried pancetta to garnish.

Chef's note: The dressing I use is a Granny Smith and basil oil one which will add a great sharpness to the dish.

THE WHITE HART HOTEL

The White Hart, 26 High Street, Dorchester-on-Thames, Oxfordshire OX10 7HN
Tel: 01865 340074
www.white-hart-hotel-dorchester.co.uk

Monkfish wrapped in prosciutto ham, creamed cabbage, saffron potatoes and asparagus cream

INGREDIENTS

Monkfish
4 x 250g monkfish
fillet, each piece
wrapped in two slices
and refrigerate
8 slices of prosciutto

Creamed cabbage
$1/_2$ Savoy cabbage,
shredded
2 cloves crushed garlic
100ml white wine
100ml double cream

2 shallots, thinly sliced
50g butter
Salt and pepper

**Asparagus cream
sauce**
1 bunch pencil-sized
asparagus – tips taken
off and kept aside, stems
chopped
1 shallot, sliced
$1/_2$ lemon, juiced
Sprig tarragon

200ml double cream
2 sliced mushrooms
50ml fish stock
25ml white wine vinegar
50g butter
Salt and pepper

Saffron potatoes
1 pinch saffron strands
500ml chicken stock
12 large new potatoes
1tsp sea salt
25g butter

METHOD

Cream cabbage
Sweat off the garlic, shallots and cabbage in the butter. Add the white wine and
reduce by two-thirds. Add the cream and reduce by half. Adjust your seasoning and
put to one side

Asparagus cream sauce
Sweat off the mushrooms, asparagus stems and shallot in half the butter. Deglaze the
pan with the wine vinegar and stock. Slowly reduce by half, then add lemon juice,
reduce again by half. Add the cream and bring to the boil. Adjust your seasoning and
leave aside for five minutes. Blitz in a food blender and pass through a chinois into a
small pan, whisk in the other half of butter.

Saffron potatoes
Turn the new potatoes into small barrel shapes. Place in a pan with the stock, saffron
and salt. Bring to the boil until tender. Remove from the heat and stir in the butter,
drop in the asparagus tips you put aside. Leave in liquid until needed.

To finish
Seal the monkfish on each side in a hot, non-stick pan with a little oil. Remove into
an oven proof dish and pour over the hot fat. Place in an oven 200°C for around six
minutes. Remove from oven and allow to rest. Reheat the cabbage, sauce and
potatoes. Push the cabbage into a ring, in the middle of the plate. Cut the monkfish
into three pieces and arrange around the cabbage. Fill the gaps with potatoes and
asparagus. Drizzle the creamy sauce around.

THE WHITE HART HOTEL

The White Hart, 26 High Street, Dorchester-on-Thames, Oxfordshire OX10 7HN
Tel: 01865 340074
www.white-hart-hotel-dorchester.co.uk

Chilled rhubarb and custard with crumble ice cream

4 eggs, separated

250ml milk

250ml double cream (semi-whipped)

250g rhubarb purée

5 gelatine leaves (soaked in cold water until soft)

150g caster sugar

8 shortbread biscuits

100g melted butter

Custard cream

10g custard powder

2 eggs

1 vanilla pod (split)

50g flour

100g caster sugar

250ml milk

250ml cream

Crumble ice cream

1 small tub of good quality vanilla ice cream

6 shortbread biscuits crushed

1tsp dark rum

Garnish

Rhubarb crisps

Mint sprigs

Raspberries

Caramel spiral (sugar and water mixture

Blitz the biscuits in processor and mix with melted butter. Push into a lined tray and refrigerate until set. Slowly bring the milk and purée to the boil. Cream together the yolks and sugar until pale. Whisk the milk on to the egg and mix well.

Return the mix into the pan and cook gently over a low heat until it coats the back of the spoon. Remove from the pan into a large bowl and whisk in the gelatine. Leave in a cool place stirring occasionally until almost setting point.

Fold in the lightly beaten cream, the stiffly beaten egg whites and pour over the biscuit mix and refrigerate.

Custard cream

Whisk together powder, flour, sugar and eggs. Boil the milk and cream with the split pod in a thick-based pan, whisk over the eggs. Return to the pan and cook until thick. Refrigerate until serving.

Crumble ice cream

Crush the biscuits in a bag with a rolling pin. Remove ice cream from tub for a couple of minutes. Lightly grill the crumbs until golden, then mix into the ice cream along with the rum. Place back in freezer.

To serve

To make the caramel spiral, boil sugar and water until golden, and working quickly before cooling, wrap around and along a sharpening steel using a dessert spoon to guide the smooth syrupy mixture.

Plate up rhubarb biscuit mix, pour over custard, serve with crumble ice cream, a caramel spiral, made by sprig of mint, three raspberries per person, rhubarb coulis and rhubarb crisps (bought).

THE WHITE HART HOTEL

The White Hart, 26 High Street, Dorchester-on-Thames, Oxfordshire OX10 7HN
Tel: 01865 340074
www.white-hart-hotel-dorchester.co.uk

CONTRIBUTORS

BROOKES
Oxford Brookes University, Gipsy Lane. Deddington,
Oxfordshire OX3 OBP
Tel: 01865 483803
www.brookes.ac.uk/restaurant

BROWNS
5-11 Woodstock Road, Oxford OX2 6HA
Tel: 01865 511995
www.browns-restaurants.com

THE DEDDINGTON ARMS
Horsefair, Deddington Oxfordshire
OX15 OSH
Tel: 01869 338364
www.deddington-arms-hotel.co.uk
www.oxford-restaurants-hotels.co.uk

THE EAGLE TAVERN
Little Coxwell, Faringdon, Oxfordshire SN7 7LW
Tel: 01367 240120
www.eagletavern.co.uk

FISHERS
36-7 St Clements, Oxford OX4 1AB
Tel: 01865 243003
www.fishers-restaurant.com

GEE'S
61 Banbury Road, Oxford OX2 6NN
Tel: 01865 553540
www.oxford-hotels-restaurants.co.uk

HAWKWELL HOUSE HOTEL
Church Way, Iffley Village, Oxford OX4 4DZ
Tel: 01865 749988
www.hawkwellhouse.co.uk

THE KAZBAR
25-7 Cowley Road, Oxford OX4 1HP
Tel: 01865 202920

THE LEMON TREE
268 Woodstock Road, Oxford OX2 7NW
Tel: 01865 311936

MEDIO
The Oxford Hotel, Godstow Road, Oxford OX2 8AL
Tel: 01865 489937
www.paramount-
hotels.co.uk/destinations/central_england/oxford

MOLE AND CHICKEN
Easington Terrace, Long Crendon, Aylesbury HP18 9EY
Tel: 01844 208387
www.moleandchicken.co.uk

OLD PARSONAGE
1 Banbury Road, Oxford OX2 6NN
Tel: 01865 310210
www.oldparsonage-hotel.co.uk
www.oxford-hotels-restaurants.co.uk

THE OLIVE
Market Place, Deddington, Oxfordshire OX15 OSE
Tel: 01869 338813
www.theoliverestaurant.co.uk

QUOD
92-94 High Street, Oxford OX1 4BN
Tel: 01865 202505

SIP RESTAURANT & BAR
102 Walton Street, Jericho, Oxford OX2 6EB
Tel: 01865 311322
www.barsip.com

SIXTY SIX A
The Cotswold Lodge Hotel
66A Banbury Road, Oxford OX2 6JP
Tel: 01865 512121
www.cotswoldlodgehotel.co.uk

THE WHITE HART HOTEL
26 High Street, Dorchester-on-Thames, Oxfordshire OX10 7HN
Tel: 01865 340074
www.white-hart-hotel-dorchester.co.uk

STORE CUPBOARD

BASICS
Rice: Basmati, arborio, brown
Mustard: Dijon, wholegrain,
mustard powder
Oils: Olive, canola, vegetable,
sesame, walnut
Vinegars: Red, white wine,
balsamic, chinese rice
Flour: Plain, self raising
Dried chillies
Bay leaves
Root ginger
Cous cous
Salt: Sea, cooking, table

Sugar: Brown, white
Tinned tomatoes
Pulses: Borlotti, cannelloni,
butter Beans, chickpeas
Lentils: Brown, red
Nuts: Cashew, pistachio,
walnut
Almonds: blanched, whole,
flaked, slivered
Coconut milk
**Cooking chocolate and cocoa
powder – 70%**
Sauces: Soya, fish, oyster
Anchovies

FRESH HERBS
Basil
Coriander
Rosemary
Thyme
Sage
Bay
Mint
Dill
Chervil

SPICES
Curry leaves
Turmeric powder

Cinnamon powder
Clove powder
Nutmeg powder
Chilli powder
Coriander powder
Cumin seeds
Coriander seeds
Cardamom pods
Fennel seeds
Mustard seeds
Caraway seeds
Peppercorns
Garam Masala
Star anise

EQUIPMENT

RECOMMENDED
Baking parchment For non-stick effect.
Cake spatula For easing out cakes from tins.
Casserole Preferably cast iron, 5 pint = family size.
Chinois Metal conical sieve with fine mesh.
Colander Metal, with handles.
Dariole Small cylindrical mould.
Digital scales Considered to be the most accurate.
Draining spoon Metal, longhandled.
Food processor Good quality multi-purpose, with blender.
Frying pan Eight inch and ten inch.
Grater Four-sided, easy to clean.
Kitchen timer With alarm mechanism.
Knife set Good quality cook's knives, serrated, bread, paring,
carving, palette, cleaver.
Large mixing bowl Plus smaller glass bowls.

Mandolin Instrument, not musical, for finely slicing.
Measuring jugs Two varying sizes.
Pastry brush For basting.
Pastry Cutters Various shapes and sizes, preferably metal.
Pestle and morter Stone, not porcelain.
Rolling pin Wooden.
Saucepans Aluminium, stainless steel, copper-based, non-stick.
Sieves Rounded/conical.
Steamer Either freestanding or saucepan top.
Sugar thermometer Essential in confectionary and some dessert
making, but also useful for fat temperature.
Tins Metal baking sheet, roasting tin, flan ring, mould, cake tins,
patty tins, spring form tin, loaf tin.
Whisk Balloon/electric.
Wooden spoons Different sizes, plus wooden spatula.

COOKING TERMS AND METHODS

Bain-Marie A cooking method where the dish is cooked immersed in a half-filled tin or pan of boiling water.

Baste To coat during cooking.

Bind To blend dry and liquid ingredients.

Blanch To briefly cook in boiling water.

Blister To heat the surface of an ingredient. For example: peppers, until the skin blisters.

Blitz To rapidly blend or heat ingredients.

Brown To cook until surface starts to brown.

Caramelise To heat sugar or sugar syrup until it browns to a caramel colour.

Chinois Very fine sieve.

Compote A thick purée of fruit.

Concasse Coarsely chopped ingredients.

Confit Meat cooked in own fat and then preserved encased in fat to prevent contact with air.

Consommé A light clear soup/sauce.

Coulis A light fruit sauce.

Croquant Biscuit, from French for crunchy or crisp.

Croustillant A dish either presented on, or enclosed in, a shell of pastry.

Debearded A term applying to preparation of shellfish, where little hairs have been removed.

Deskirted Another shellfish term referring to trimming and cleaning of scallops.

Deglaze To heat a liquid, usually stock or wine, with pan juices as basis for gravy.

Demiglace Rich, concentrated brown stock, can be bought ready-made.

Dice Finely chop.

Flambé To flame a mixture containing alcohol.

Flash-fry To quickly fry.

Fold To gently combine ingredients with a metal spoon or knife.

Glaze To coat food with egg, milk or syrup before or after cooking.

Infuse To immerse strong flavoured ingredients in hot liquid, which is then left to stand for a while eg vanilla pods in milk.

Jus A clear stock or pure fruit juice.

Knead A technique applied in perfecting dough, done by hand on a floured board.

Macerate To steep in alcohol or syrup, in order to flavour or soften.

Marinade A mixture in which meat, fish or other ingredients are soaked before cooking.

Napping To coat an item with sauce.

Noisette Small piece of meat, usually the eye of a chop.

Parboil To partly boil, from five to 15 minutes.

Poach To cook food at just below boiling point for a protracted time.

Prove The second stage in bread making, where dough is allowed to rise after shaping.

Refresh Plunging just boiled or blanched vegetables into cold water, to preserve fresh colour.

Rillette A coarse paté.

Roux The butter and flour base to sauces – flour is added to melted butter and cooked into a paste for a minute before adding liquid.

Reduce To boil rapidly to reduce liquid content and concentrate flavour.

Sauté To lightly fry.

Sear To rapidly pan-cook meat at a high temperature.

Strain To pass liquid through a sieve to free it of lumps.

Sweat To seal in a covered pan.

Terrine A layered and set loaf-shaped starter, often incorporating meat.

Turn To shape with a knife or peeler, whilst rotating, into a regular, round shape.

Whipping To beat quickly with a spoon or whisk to incorporate air.

GLOSSARY

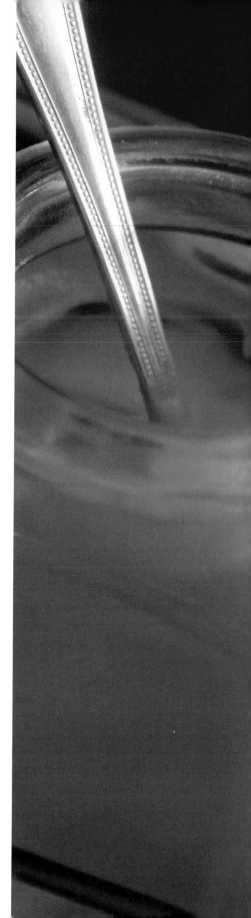

Allspice berry From the West Indian allspice tree. When ground, it has the aroma and taste of a combination of cinnamon, cloves, nutmeg and pepper.

Borlotti bean A large, plump bean, pinkish brown in colour with reddish brown streaks, available dried or tinned. Widely used in Italian cooking.

Cardamon The seeds are contained in small pods, which you crush to remove the seeds. Strong aroma and a warm, spicy-sweet flavour.

Cane syrup Golden syrup.

Capers Pickled flower buds of a shrub native to the Mediterranean and parts of Asia. Usually bought in jars.

Chervil An aromatic herb, like tarragon, with lacy leaves.

Chilli oil Bought ready-bottled from supermarkets.

Chinese wine Available from Chinese supermarkets. Use dry sherry as substitute.

Chorizo A Spanish sausage, spicy in flavour and made of ground pork.

Celeriac Root vegetable cooked like potato, with distinctive celery taste.

Cinnamon sticks Cinnamon bark in stick form, available from good supermarkets.

Cous cous A fine cereal made from semolina.

Five spice powder Chinese spice containing cinnamon, cloves, fennel, star anise and Sichuan peppers.

Harrisa North African hot paste.

Kirsch A liqueur distilled from crushed cherries and their stones.

Lardons Small, chunky strips – usually of bacon or pork.

Lemon grass Stalk used in Chinese and Thai cookery. Discard outer husk and crush inner stem for lemon flavour.

Mache A green salad leaf native to Europe with dark green leaves and tangy flavour. Also called field salad, field lettuce and lamb's lettuce.

Maris Piper Versatile, good quality potato.

Mange tout Whole pea pods, eaten young and blanched.

Manzanilla A very dry, pale sherry from Spain.

Marsala Fortified wine produced in Marsala, Sicily.

Mascarpone Italian soft cheese, often used in desserts.

Pak choy Chinese cabbage with a mild mustard taste.

Port wine sauce A traditional, rich sauce that can be bought ready-prepared.

Root ginger Thick root of a tropical plant, can be frozen.

Saffron Vibrant natural colorant, extracted from crocuses.

Salmon keta A small salmon, native to the Pacific Coast of America.

Saltpeter Potassium nitrate, used in preservation of meat. Available from chemists or online.

Savoyarde biscuits Traditional dessert biscuits, readily available.

Scallops Shellfish available in a range of sizes, with delicate taste.

Soy sauce Made from fermented soy beans. Use dark for extra colour, light for flavour and salty taste.

Star anise Star-shaped seed pods with distinctive taste, available from Chinese supermarkets.

Tuile A French biscuit, moulded into curved shape while still hot.

Turmeric Spice used in Indian cooking, mainly for its bright yellow colour.

Vanilla pod Fragrant dried pods of the vanilla orchid.

CONVERSION TABLES

TEMPERATURE

GAS	ELECTRIC DEGREES F	ELECTRIC DEGREES C
1	275	140 very cool
2	300	150 cool
3	325	170 warm
4	350	180 moderate
5	375	190 fairly hot
6	400	200 hot
7	425	220 very hot
8	450	230 very hot
9	475	240 very hot

WEIGHTS

1oz	25g
2	50g
3	75g
4	110g
5	150g
6	175g
7	200g
8	225g
9	250g
10	275g
12	350g
1lb	450g
1.5lb	700g
2lb	900g
3lb	1.3kg

LIQUIDS

2fl oz	60ml
3	90ml
5	150ml
10	300ml
15	450ml
1 pint	600ml
1.25	750ml
1.75	1 litre
2	1.2
2.5	1.5

INDEX OF RECIPES BY COURSE

DESSERTS

TAPAS

NOTES

Notes